Leading with Compassion

Business schools teach the transactional tools one needs to work in business. They teach various strategic planning and decision-making models such as SPACE or SWOT or decision trees or weighted grids. They teach about the various functions of an organization, financial ratios, and breakeven analyses. And they may even have a class on business ethics. But those tools are more about knowing where the business-case boundaries are as a risk prevention measure and do not help one to think about how they should comport themselves as a leader.

This book is about helping you to become your best self and helping those around you to achieve their best. Inherently it's about authenticity, integrity, and empathy and how these simple traits can lead to high performance. The book explores ways to make our leadership more authentic and to lead with integrity. It discusses how to mentor employees and how this can lead to higher-performing teams and more successful organizations.

The book is organized around four major constructs. The first is about personal leadership. It starts with honesty and integrity. That provides the basis for an empathetic leadership style. This is one that helps to engage followers and brings them along because they want to come along for the journey, rather than feeling forced. That is the nature of the second construct: building and maintaining high-performing teams. This is then the basis for building a trusting culture. Change is all around us and that can be exhausting. Building a culture of trust is the first step toward building an agile organizational culture. That is the third construct. Finally, the last is a message of simple optimism. There are many challenges facing society today, but with thoughtful, engaging leaders there is hope that we can collectively rise to the challenge.

Leading with Compassion

How to Make Leadership Authentic by Managing with Integrity

Dr. Gregory E. Worden

Routledge
Taylor & Francis Group

A PRODUCTIVITY PRESS BOOK

First published 2023
by Routledge
605 Third Avenue, New York, NY 10158

and by Routledge
4 Park Square, Milton Park, Abingdon, Oxon, OX14 4RN

Routledge is an imprint of the Taylor & Francis Group, an informa business

ISBN: 9781032347882 (hbk)
ISBN: 9781032347851 (pbk)
ISBN: 9781003323853 (ebk)

DOI: 10.4324/9781003323853

Typeset in Garamond
by Deanta Global Publishing Services, Chennai, India

Thank you to my dear friends in the First Congregational
Church of Camden, Maine, for their trust, support,
curiosity, and for those frustrating moments
when they pushed me to be my better self.

But especially thank you to my wife, Vicki, for saying, "stop
telling me these stories and write a book about them instead."

Huge thanks also to my good friends, Dr. Todd Kelley
and Dr. Dawn Edmiston. I had attended the University
of Maryland Global Campus with both of them and
came to know them as smart, capable, thoughtful, and
caring people. They both gave me the "tough love" that
I needed to take this from a rough concept to a finished
book. I hope my writing has done them a fine service.

Contents

Preface

This is meant to be a fun, engaging read for leaders at all levels, whether you hold a title or you lead by example. It is not academic, but I do draw from academic literature to support my assertions. This isn't a comprehensive guide to all things leadership. That would be a massive undertaking. Rather this is meant to be an inspirational guide.

The book is organized around four major constructs. The first is about personal leadership. It starts with honesty and integrity. That provides the basis for an empathetic leadership style. This is one that helps to engage followers and brings them along because they want to come along for the journey rather than feeling forced. That is the nature of the second construct: building and maintaining high-performing teams. This is then the basis for building a trusting culture. Change is all around us and that can be exhausting. Building a culture of trust is the first step toward building an agile organizational culture. That is the third construct. Finally, the last is a message of simple optimism. There are many challenges facing society today, but with thoughtful, engaging leaders, there is hope that we can collectively rise to the challenge. Change can indeed be exhausting, but it can also be a lot of fun.

The examples I use come from a combination of my experience teaching at the graduate level, my business experience, and my experience as a lay leader in a church. The latter was surprisingly more challenging than business, and that had a way of clarifying and highlighting many of the concepts that I discuss here. I hope you enjoy the book.

About the Author

Dr. Greg Worden grew up in a congregational church in western New York. He holds a bachelor's degree in aerospace engineering, a master's in information technology systems management, and a doctorate in international operations. He worked for several years as a contractor to NASA Goddard Space Flight Center on earth-remote sensing satellites before moving on to a career consulting for several Federal Government agencies. He has worked in enterprise architecture, business process reengineering, and strategic planning and later was the CEO of a wind energy company. He has taught at multiple universities at all three levels. He's currently working on several budding and interesting projects.

Chapter 1

Introduction

This book is about helping you to become your best self and helping those around you to achieve their best. Inherently it's about authenticity, integrity, and empathy and how these simple traits can lead to high performance. It is unabashedly aspirational. It's not the way the world always works. It's the way the world should work, and it's the way I teach about it in Sunday School. Please come on this journey with me.

In business school, we teach the transactional tools one needs to work in business. We teach various strategic planning and decision-making models such as SPACE or SWOT or decision trees or weighted grids. We teach about the various functions of an organization. We teach financial ratios and breakeven analyses. We may even have a class on business ethics. But those tools are more about knowing where the business-case boundaries are as a risk prevention measure and do not help one to think about how they should comport themselves as a leader. There is usually a leadership class somewhere in the mix where we teach and learn about the traditional leadership models such as charismatic or the contingency theory of leadership. These concepts and tools are valuable. Indeed, they are even necessary, but they are not sufficient.

DOI: 10.4324/9781003323853-1

In this book, we'll explore ways to make our leadership more authentic and to lead with integrity. We'll discuss how to mentor our employees and how this can lead to higher-performing teams and more successful organizations. You can guess from the title that lessons will be drawn from church. But don't fear, even if you are not a church-going person, you'll find a lot of valuable information here. This is not a preachy book, and you are also free to disagree with my conclusions.

You can read this book in one of two ways. You can read this as a general book about leadership applicable to any organization. Or you can read this as a church leader hoping to improve your leadership skills in your church life. In fact, those new to church leadership will indeed find this book useful.

It's important at this point that I clarify my terms. This book is aimed at leadership in any type of organization, whether business, not-for-profit, volunteer, or otherwise. As such I naturally switch between the terms "organizational life," "business life," or "professional life." For all intents and purposes, they mean the same thing. During the drafting process, I tried to normalize the terms but that only made reading more awkward so please view this book as leadership lessons for all types of organizations.

There are a lot of books written about leadership lessons from Jesus or the Bible. This book is not intended to duplicate those works. Rather this is about drawing lessons from working in church life as a lay leader. Working in a church is surprisingly difficult. For many of us our experience with church life may be only through the prism of Sunday service or weddings or funerals. But being a volunteer or a leader in a church is far more complicated than it might at first appear. There are several reasons for this, but one key reason is that church leaders are expected to be held to a higher standard. Certainly, there are countless cases of abuse or corruption from church leaders but there are also countless lay leaders (those who are not members of the clergy) who do strive to meet those higher standards. This is in a large part why this book is important: to help you reach that higher standard and inspire those around you.

Church life also presages the way general organizational life is changing. For instance, while working in church committees, it is common to work with a multigenerational team ranging all the way from teenagers to people in their nineties. In many organizations, people are working longer into their 70s and 80s and hence increasingly organizations are multigenerational. Churches and organizations in general may have different missions and goals, but the way we work within each is surprisingly similar.

But before we go into the details, it's useful to set the stage.

Everything in church life is emotional. We're dealing with life, death, the meaning of life, how we should live our life, is there an afterlife, as well as tradition and history. These items strike deep into our emotions and our psyche. For many, religion is a core part of their identity, even if they don't consider themselves religious or actively practice religion. Messing with that identity can instantly incite inner crisis and turmoil. Even comparatively simple decisions can become hotbeds for strife.

But before we discuss conflict, it's important to set the stage with some background. I was a lay leader in a congregational church in New England. Congregational churches draw their inspiration from the Pilgrims. When they settled in New England, they brought their seeds of democracy. They were fleeing the aristocracy and hierarchy of England and Europe. Theirs was to be a new way founded on the principles of equality. They did not want to be told what to do but rather decide for themselves through discussion and voting. They chose their minister rather than having one imposed from above, as was the case previously. Modern congregational churches follow this model. The members of the church run the church, and the minister is meant to be a partner. When the congregation decides the minister has become stale and should move on, they can make that decision. This level of equality is wonderful but also fraught with potential conflict.

A core tenant of this book is that management does not have to be management by conflict but rather management of conflict. Business schools don't teach management by conflict explicitly but often implicitly. I can remember consulting on a Federal Government contract working with one of the largest information technology companies in the country, and the pervasive management style was by conflict. Decisions were made by shouting. The one who shouted the loudest and longest won the meeting. The consequence of that was extreme inefficiency as few in the meeting "bought into" the decision. So, resistance became the norm. More shouting ensued, followed by stubborn acceptance.

But organizations don't have to be that way. Successful managers are able to get the best out of each individual person. They recognize their talents. When conflict inevitably occurs – it's natural and nothing to be worried about – the best managers are able to bring the team together and positively make a decision, achieving buy in. When all members of the team are onboard – or at least most of the team – then the team can perform.

It's imperative to remember that conflict will occur, and we shouldn't avoid it. In fact, one lesson from church life is that avoidance is seriously detrimental. Church members want to be seen as, if not pious, good people. Therefore, they don't want to argue nastily with each other at least publicly. Behind closed doors or over email or social media the arguments fester. Pockets of division and discord are sewed. Then when the problems do come to light, the battle lines are drawn. This is the negative side of the conflict, and in church life it immediately leads to suboptimal solutions, lack of buy in, and inefficiency. This is particularly acute in church life as the members may simply leave. There is a central tenant in church life that every member is valued. Leaving is painful for everyone involved. Yelling may work, albeit poorly, in business – and there is a time and place for it – but yelling at volunteers means they won't be volunteers any longer.

But volunteering in a church also brings other, unique challenges. We may find ourselves working in a committee or team ranging from teenagers up to people in their nineties. These are extreme examples of multigenerational workplaces. Each generation has a slightly different worldview that impacts their decision-making. They also have a different view and capability when it comes to technology. Then we may also find that we have a wide variety of backgrounds with a wide variety of educations. I led a team with schoolteachers, lawyers, the former CEO of a local hospital, artists, and a massage therapist. They were all wonderful people but had such diverse backgrounds that I had to be very deliberate in my communications. My go-to organizational tool is a Gantt chart. I was the only one who knew what that was. I prefer to keep everything electronic on a shared website. Some of my team didn't own a computer. It was a challenge but one worth undertaking, and the results were wonderful.

One may be tempted to think that this is unique to a church and hence of no importance to broader organizations. But organizations are changing. People are living longer and working longer. It's not unusual to see people working into their 70s and soon their 80s. Retire at 65? What does retirement mean? For many it means continuing to work, perhaps not 60 hours a week, but continuing on. I've heard from some people that they are concerned that retirement may lead to cognitive loss and so they stay working. Working in this context can mean many things. Sometimes it will mean staying on in the same job or in a slightly different position, or it may mean part-time jobs or volunteer positions. Many organizations have a mix of full-time and part-time staff and volunteers.

Not only are multigenerational workplaces the norm and the number of generations in the workplace is increasing, but change can be complicated by this. Change in a church environment is especially difficult. I successfully managed a major organizational culture change in such an environment, and I learned humility, transparency, and most of all – patience. These are tools that are useful for managers anywhere.

During this change in the management process, I used the principles of a simple but powerful change management methodology called Appreciative Inquiry. This is a well-known change management tool that can be used in nearly any type of organization. It's particularly useful in an emotionally charged or politically sensitive environment. The process starts off with ground rules: we're going to focus on the positives and the future. We will not focus on the problems. Once people agree to these rules – really agree not just a nodding agreement – then they collectively plan for the future, and once everyone is working together, all those problems that perhaps got us to this point surprisingly get solved because now everyone is working together instead of at cross purposes.

As part of the change management process, we entered into a purposeful discernment. This is where we ask ourselves why we exist in the first place and where we want to go in the future. In the corporate world, this is called strategic planning and visioning. Company executives might look at the company mission and vision statements, tweak some words, and then set some new performance targets for the next five years. What we do in a church is similar but far deeper and more meaningful. We focus on the question: why do we exist in the first place? Then, how do we connect with each other and the community? Then we ask where we want to go in the future. This is inherently deeper than a standard strategic planning process.

Interestingly, there is a discipline called stakeholder management that many in the organization world would recognize. This is how the organizations work with and communicate with everyone on which they have an impact and who has an impact on the organization. Stakeholders would be employees, government entities, the community in which the company does business, customers, and more. A subset of this discipline is called *normative stakeholder analysis*. This is a deep look at why the organization exists, and it's meant to be honest. The organization may indeed exist to make the owner as much money as possible in a particular field. That's not what most mission statements would say! Taking this a few layers deeper may lead executives to begin to think about the impact the company has on the world around them and how they can make that impact more meaningful. Certainly, launching a product in a new color next year might be a good idea but can we instead look at how we can launch a product that makes peoples' lives better or reduces pollution? Normative stakeholder analysis can take us in that direction.

Before delving into the following chapters, it should be said at the outset that I use the term "manager" and "leader" interchangeably throughout this book. Academics will say there is a difference, and while true, it is, well, academic. A person with the title "manager" may "manage" employees by assigning tasks or reviewing expense reports. That same manager may then "lead" employees by inspiring and motivating them to higher levels of performance. So, for our purposes here, a manager will both manage and lead and hence there is no need to differentiate.

Further, it's appropriate to recognize that while there are indeed many lessons to be learned from church life, I fully note that terrible things have been done and continue to be done in the name of religion. I don't pretend, in any way, that religion is perfect or provides all answers to all questions nor will I be so egotistical as to propose that congregationalism is a better denomination than any other. Congregational churches are fiercely independent, and matters of faith will differ from one church to another. The historic origins of the church are interesting, and toward the end of the book I provide a little background on this. I talk about congregationalism because that is my background and my life in that church's leadership is from where I developed the lessons we'll discuss next.

Organization of the Book

The book is structured around four major sections. The first section is a personal reflection of what it means to be a leader and the type of leadership needed today. This foundation – leading with authenticity and integrity – sets the stage for the next section. Leveraging this personal foundation we can begin to meaningfully shape our staff and those around us, leading to high-performing teams. This then builds momentum to think meaningfully about the way the organization functions, which in turn leads us to think about the role of the organization and our ability to rise to the challenges of the 21st century.

Chapter 2

First Help Yourself

Lay leaders in churches are held to a different standard than their counterparts in business, or at least should be. Everything in church life is inherently emotional. Churches are dealing with the biggest issues: birth, death, whether there is an afterlife, and the meaning of life. Churches help to bind us both to the past and to the future. They are bastions of calm in the midst of the craziness of life outside. Even then, navigating these emotional waters is surprisingly challenging.

Our church deacons recently decided to change the way communion was served. Rather than bringing the bread and wine to each seated member, the deacons asked the members to come to the front of the sanctuary to receive the bread and wine. This is called communion by intinction. This was met with a firestorm of anger. Our choir recently decided to stop wearing choir robes during the summer because they were hot. This was met with a firestorm of anger. Our Sunday School director decided to change the Sunday School curriculum. Yes, this too was met with a firestorm of anger. All of the changes were small and none changed the deeper meaning of the ritual but because the members felt bound by the history, change was extremely hard. That bastion of calm was at risk.

DOI: 10.4324/9781003323853-2

Lay leaders or even church staff who are new to this reality are often shocked. A new lay leader will be transitioning from being just a member to bearing the brunt of the anger. Navigating this successfully means leading with authenticity and leading with integrity. It also means leading with patience, but that's obvious, right?

As I mentioned at the outset of this book, every church denomination is different. Some may indeed be very hierarchical or run by a charismatic leader or one who leads by decree or perhaps one who is very politically savvy and can convince and cajole members to follow along much the same way a politician running for office would. For any right way to do something, there is always a wrong way that may also succeed in the short run. There are countless examples of terrible people getting ahead and that's certainly true in church life too. There are books such as Machiavelli's infamous *The Prince*. There Machiavelli counseled new royalty to lead according to political necessity and expediency and ignore morality as the guiding principle. But one would expect a book about church life applied to organizational life to be the opposite and hence we'll look at the morally right way to be a leader both in church life and business life and, by extension, in life in general.

Authenticity and Integrity

Leading with authenticity and integrity is precisely the opposite of Machiavelli's advice. Let's start with authenticity. Stewart Friedman of the University of Pennsylvania's Wharton School of Business defines authenticity as:

> Authenticity (or being real) arises when leaders behave in ways that are consistent with their core values. Leaders must define and articulate a vision

that embraces the diverse values and lifestyle of all employees. Their everyday actions must fit with not only their personal values but also with the core values of the business. They must delegate to cultivate trust, build on strengths, and increase commitment to shared goals through genuine dialogue with key stakeholders, the people about whom they care most, in all life domains.*

Authors, John Sosik and Weichun Zhu from the Pennsylvania State University add to this by noting that authenticity manifests itself in several roles: visionary, positive role model, champion of change, coach/mentor.† Authentic leaders must not only see political expediency but rather embrace the larger view and act according to consistent values. They must demonstrate positive rather than negative traits and model proper behavior at all times but especially in times of change and stress. They must also recognize how difficult change will be and provide that steadfastness and strength of character that when minor issues turn into firestorms, they are able to calmly help members work through their anger, grief, confusion, joy, and all the other feelings that get exposed during times of change. They must listen. They must accept diverse viewpoints as real, not imagined. They must also seek to build trust and increase commitment to shared goals. That is the role of a coach and mentor.

Undoubtedly this is not easy. It's far easier to simply get angry and resort to expedient means. You don't like the new curriculum? Well, we voted and we're doing it anyway. Tough. Machiavelli would likely approve but the tricky thing

---

* https://knowledge.wharton.upenn.edu/article/cultivating-total-leadership-with-authenticity-integrity-and-creativity/
† John Sosik and Weichun Zhu, *Felt Authenticity and Demonstrating Transformational Leadership in Faith Communities,* The Pennsylvania State University, 2011, Institute of Behavioral and Applied Management.

about church members is that angry church members are not members very long. In business it's easy to simply hand the orders down and move on, but if you want buy-in, consistent performance from your employees, and high-performing teams, it's better to do things right rather than fast.

Here however, we enter into a bit of a muddle. Friedman defined authenticity above and other academics will broadly agree, but this is imperfect. When we think about politics, it's common to hear voters claim that one candidate is more authentic than the other. They are true to their core values. They don't speak politically correctly. They don't filter their words and statements to avoid causing offense. They call it like they see it.

Some of most crass politicians have been labeled authentic because they swear, curse, denigrate one or more groups, routinely hurl insults at the other side, play fast and loose with the truth, and more. They are the opposite of politically correct. They are unvarnished. They are labeled authentic. Machiavelli would be proud. But it's my turn to write a book.

Authenticity clearly cannot be enough. Integrity is required. We turn back to Friedman:

> Integrity (or being whole) arises when the different aspects of life fit together coherently and consistently. How do leaders achieve this? They must take responsibility for capturing synergies across all aspects of their lives – at work, at home, in the community and in themselves (their health, spiritual growth, and leisure). They must align the interests of different stakeholders in the pursuit of collective goals as well as set, maintain, and respect the boundaries that enable value to be created at work and in other aspects of their lives. And they must invest in social capital to nurture networks and partnerships that provide the support needed for achieving results that matter.

Integrity is often synonymous with honesty and while indeed that is the first principle of integrity, it's also about being whole. This means that one cannot be honest in one instance and not the next. It's about being honest and transparent in all areas of one's life. Church members will quickly lose trust in a lay leader if they see them acting pious at church and crass at the ball game swearing at the Little League umpires. True integrity arises through consistent honesty and transparency.

As Friedman notes, however, integrity impacts the way we work with different people and groups – to align the stakeholders and work toward collective goals. As I mentioned in the beginning of this chapter, patience is required. Integrity is the reason why. It's far easier to take the shortcut and get things done quickly and move on to something else. Church leaders are supposed to be held to impeccable standards. Hence, when confronted by angry parents that a Sunday School curriculum may change, it's imperative to listen to each of the viewpoints, discuss the collective goals, and nurture the network and partnership. This takes time and commitment. It takes integrity. It takes patience.

Quiet Ego

A crucial part of this is understanding oneself in the role of one's ego. It is through the ego that we seek self-affirmation. Clearly, this can help us to perform better. A salesperson may wish to work harder and sell more not only to read the material benefits of sales commissions but also to feel better about themselves. An athlete, similarly, may work harder on the field to score more goals not only to help the team succeed but also perhaps to help them win a personal trophy for the most goals scored in a season. Without a doubt this type of self-affirmation is healthy. But, not surprisingly, there is a downside to too much ego.

The downside of too much ego may mean that in one's quest for self-affirmation one may be so concerned about themselves that they sacrifice friendships and relationships as a result. Worse, seeking that self-affirmation may mean defending bad decisions when honest acknowledgment would ultimately be better.

In financial trading, there is a phrase called revenge trading. The notion is that when a trader makes a bad trade and loses money, they want to quickly make that money back so they make another trade even bigger than the last one to get revenge over their own bad decision. The downside is that they often end up losing even more money, hence the need for the phrase.

We also see this in politics all too frequently. Rather than acknowledge that the other side actually has some good ideas, it becomes a zero-sum game where each side tries to denigrate the other and win at all costs. When we can no longer recognize that other people also have value in our political discourse, the response is a descent into name-calling for which we are all worse off.

As Scott Barry Kaufman writes in his 2018 article, "The Pressing Need for Everyone to Quiet Their Egos":

> Conversely, when we can rein in our ego and recognize the value in other people's ideas and take time to consider multiple perspectives rather than subverting our own goals, we may find that we achieve them more easily in a way that is more enduring. The term for this is called the quiet ego. [Other researchers] have been developing a "quiet ego" research program grounded in Buddhist philosophy and humanistic psychology ideals and backed by empirical research in the field of positive psychology. Paradoxically, it turns out that quieting the ego is so much more effective in cultivating well-being,

growth, health, productivity, and a healthy, productive self-esteem, than focusing so loudly on self enhancement.*

At this point you may be tempted to wonder why a book originally inspired by Congregationalism is taking cues from Buddhist philosophy but isn't that a great example of a quiet ego? Again, from Kaufmann:

> The goal of the quiet ego approach is to arrive at a less defensive, and more integrative stance toward the self and others, not lose your sense of self or deny your need for the esteem from others. You can very much cultivate an authentic identity that incorporates others without losing the self or feeling the need for narcissistic displays of winning. A quiet ego is an indication of a healthy self-esteem, one that acknowledges one's own limitations, doesn't need to constantly resort to defensiveness whenever the ego is threatened, and yet has a firm sense of self-worth and competence.†

Kaufman notes the quiet ego consists of four interconnected facets: detached awareness, inclusive identity, perspective taking, and growth mindedness. The first facet is about introspection, meaning one's ability to understand one's own thoughts, feelings, and actions in terms of the larger whole. For instance, in group dynamics when the group is not performing well or is in conflict, it's important for each

---

* Scott Barry Kaufman, The Pressing Need for Everyone to Quiet Their Egos: Why Quieting the Ego Strengthens Your Best Self, *Scientific American Blogs*, May 21, 2018.
† Scott Barry Kaufman, The Pressing Need for Everyone to Quiet Their Egos: Why Quieting the Ego Strengthens Your Best Self, *Scientific American Blogs,* May 21, 2018.

member of the group to take a moment and ask themselves what exactly is their role. Are they the one who is trying to get their own way at the expense of the others? Or are they the moderator trying to help everyone see each other's positions?

When we can take time to do this, especially in a conflict situation, it's remarkable how we can then re-orient our own energies into positive actions. Often, this will help the group to get out of the storming stage and back into the norming and performing stages.

The second facet, inclusive identity, refers to the way that we take time to understand the perspective of others and to be cooperative and compassionate toward others. This fits in nicely with the third facet, perspective taking, in which we quiet our own ego and need for self-affirmation and hence we are able to understand the perspectives of others and therefore have a greater and more inclusive understanding. The final facet, growth mindedness, is perhaps the linchpin that holds the other three together. Here is the notion that growth and success are not the result of quashing others but rather understanding that personal success is entwined with the larger group's success. This notion of growth mindedness is also tied into looking at the long-term impacts rather than merely the short term.

A good manager will not only seek to quiet their own egos but to engender this throughout the organization. This will clearly lead to greater cohesion, group decision-making, and can enhance overall organizational performance. There is clearly time for a loud ego – when rapid decision-making is needed – and clearly time for a quiet ego. That sounds like a Buddhist notion doesn't it?

Let's illustrate this with an example from church life. In a congregational church where we all seek to be partners together it is imperative to listen to the views of others. In seeking to be our better selves it's also critical to examine one's thoughts, feelings, and actions as part of the greater organization. It is not necessarily expedient or easy, but it does indeed lead to greater cohesion and performance overall. For instance, I had a volunteer who had an important "officer" role in our organization. As we neared our annual meeting and had to complete our reports to present them to the congregation, she waited until the last minute just before we published the report and she provided us with reports where she re-labeled many critical items, including names of funds, such that we could make neither heads nor tails of her report. It appeared that she did this so that she would be difficult to replace, after all, no one else could possibly step in if only one person understood the critical information on which we were all relying.

Many other co-leaders were furious and spoke with me about the need for this person's immediate removal. This was almost a last straw. Unfortunately, other factors needed consideration and dealing with this individual as a human first and considering their needs, not just our anger, was essential. I was among a few that knew that this person was recovering from cancer and that this position was truly meaningful to her and helped her to be positive in her recovery. Therefore, while I agreed that she should be removed, I refused to do so until a time when the transition could be less emotional and not based on the anger of the moment. It was only a few more months until she was in a better place allowing me to have the conversation on creating a transition and allowing a new leader to be appointed to that role. She was thankful for the time that she was given and when people realized that I was addressing the performance issues but unwilling to sacrifice the long-term good of the person, then they were able to temper their frustration and work together for the greater short- and long-term good.

Strategic Listening

The key there was that I listened to and internalized the message from her. In business, it's very common to hear but not listen. How many staff meetings have you attended where the manager goes around the room and each person reports out what they have accomplished and what they hope to accomplish? Typically, when you're waiting for it to be your turn to speak you're concentrating on what you're about to say as opposed to listening to what others have to say around you. Staff meetings, along with the dreaded performance appraisals, are too often pro forma and perfunctory. Rarely are they insightful, meaningful, or even actionable. Listening is an art that too many don't practice.

All too often we think that a leader's job is to tell people what to do and what to think. Leaders should be action oriented and move fast. The best leaders bark orders and run from meeting to meeting working long hours. Some of the best leaders do indeed do that, but those are the exceptions rather than the rule.

Several years ago, I was working as a government contractor for the Federal Government and a man named Jerry was my manager. This was Jerry's model. Jerry never stopped to talk. Instead he would walk down the hallway barking at people as he went and swiftly move on to attend the next meeting. At those meetings he would shout over the top of others. That was partially Jerry's personality, but it was also the culture of the organization. Meetings were very loud and rarely productive. After the meeting when we went back to our cubicles we would pretend to be on the phone when Jerry came by or we would fabricate meetings ourselves and hide in a spare conference room until he was gone. It was a terribly inefficient and ineffective organization as a result. Jerry got attention but he didn't get results. He also had a tendency to churn through employees. Hiring and training new employees is considerably more expensive than retaining one's staff.

Strategic listening is a needed skill in modern organizational life. One's staff will have skills, background, experience, and ideas that can be very helpful to the success of the organization. It's not just up to the manager to come up with ideas. In 1994 Henry Mintzberg, a professor of business, noticed that there is the normal top-down strategy generated by executives and hopefully executed by the employees but there is also a second kind he called emergent. "An emergent strategy is a pattern of action that develops over time in an organization in the absence of a specific mission and goals, or despite a mission and goals."* The idea is that employees who are on the front line dealing with customers have ideas of their own and gradually work to make the organization successful. New opportunities may be seen and an agile organization may see a new strategy develop from the bottom up in addition to a top-down strategy. The successful manager listens to employees to understand and cultivate this emergent strategy in addition to the traditional planning.

Part of this strategic listening is to quiet one's own ego and to listen with humility in the recognition that others have something important to say as well. Kay Lindahl in her book, *The Sacred Art of Listening*, puts it this way:

> Listening with humility removes the urgent tug that we sometimes feel for conclusion and resolution in our conversations. When we learn to listen from the point of interconnectedness and service we truly hear what is said, rather than listening only long enough to give our response. Imagine a world with that kind of support. This quality is embedded in deep listening.

(p. 48)

---

* http://interactioninstitute.org/emergent-strategy/

Imagine a world with that kind of support. That's certainly different than what passes for political discourse most of the time. But beyond that this is a quality within an organization that should be vital. Not only will this help to uncover potential new ideas for an emergent strategy but it will also help you to connect more deeply with your employees.
In this way you'll be able to play the role as mentor helping them to overcome their challenges and reach their full potential in the service of the organization. This is a way of helping you to be your best self and simultaneously helping your employees to be their best. "Without inner harmony, we cannot listen to others with undivided attention and presence" (p. 54).

Strategic listening is also a way of helping the organization to become more cohesive and integrated and to accept change and become more agile. There will always be some organizations for which change is not a constant but these will be the minority rather than the norm. A barbershop, perhaps, is an organization for which there will be minimal change year over year, but any more complex organization – even a church – will need to be prepared for constant change. From Lindahl again:

> And yet the sacred art of listening is all about change. Creating something that didn't exist before cannot happen without change. Any new relationship or opportunity for listening generates change … When we find ourselves thinking we have to do things a certain way, or here ourselves saying, "That's not the way we do it here" or "it's not going to work," stop and ask the question. Is it really true, or are we simply uncomfortable with a change? Listening creatively happens when we open our hearts to others in wonder, appreciation, and all. Entering any new relationship opens us to change,

two. A whole new world of freedom, possibility, and creativity emerges when we can listen to change.[*]

(p. 102)

I can attest personally to how powerful this is. I led our congregation through an organizational change management exercise over the course of a year to prepare us for a new minister after the prior, long-serving minister had left. The first thing my team did was to embark on a listening tour. Rather than dictating to the congregation how things would be different in the future, we held a series of small group meetings in which we simply listened to peoples' fears, concerns, and hopes. We started that way in simple recognition of the fact that we all approach change in different ways. Some of us choose to cling to past worldviews while others are ready to shed those worldviews and grasp new possibilities no matter where they may lead. But the simple art of strategic listening helps to calm the fears — not erase them — and prepare people for the coming changes. This also established a deep rapport between me and the other leaders in the broader congregation. The listening didn't stop with those small group meetings but rather the strategic listening happened every day whether in the church, in the parking lot, at the grocery store, or wherever we met.

Our goal was not only to prepare the organization for change by promoting cohesion but also to make strategic listening an ongoing habit. In a congregation when one minister leaves, there is often a period of transition and then a new minister is called. There is change during the transition and there is additional change when the new minister arrives. This is often a time of concern and fear and because it may take a number of years for strategic listening

---

[*] Kay Lindahl, *The Sacred Art of Listening: Forty Reflections for Cultivating a Spiritual Practice*, Skylight Paths Publishing, Woodstock, VT, 2013.

to become embedded not only in the leadership but also in each other. Members who are not in the leadership were encouraged to listen to each other as well. Clearly, this can be true of employees in a business. Change is constant, and it's imperative that the employees not only support each other but also listen to those key ideas that may help weather the change and promote organizational success.

Patience

In business, we think in terms of time is money. We have to constantly move quickly to get the jump on the competition. This is true of course but there are also times when it's imperative to slow down and be patient. Think in terms of staff development. If you've taken the time to advertise for a position, hired a person, and trained them you've invested significant amount of time and hence money. At that point, it's important to continue to invest in staff development as opposed to churning through employees with all of the associated expense.

Staff development is more than sending employees to training programs. It's certainly much more than a performance appraisal. The latter is ostensibly for the purposes of helping the employee to know what they are doing right and wrong and where they can improve and set goals for the next year. But does that really help? Why only once a year? In my experience, performance appraisals are used as paper trails to justify low raises and/or laying off employees. In the first five years of my career as an aerospace engineer working as a contractor to NASA, I witnessed 22 layoffs and one company going out of business. I even had a friend who had a brain tumor and was out of work for a considerable period of time. He was let go. When he tried to sue, out came the performance appraisals. He was let go for "performance reasons." Yes, I'm cynical about performance appraisals. Proper staff development means working with employees as often as possible.

I remember a particular situation many years ago while still working as an engineer. I was the leader of a group of engineers ranging in age from the early twenties to sixties. I was well qualified for the job and all of the staff were amiable and friendly. I began noticing a pattern. I would make a suggestion to the team and I would be ignored. One of the team members was a friend of mine from a previous project. His name was Stan. He was in his early sixties. He and I would often talk over coffee and I would sometimes run my ideas by him before telling the larger group. On more than one occasion Stan introduced the ideas to the team before I was ready to present them. The team jumped on my ideas and ran with them. I knew Stan was not trying to steal credit. He was merely talking, and the ideas simply flowed into the conversation.

One day my manager who was located in a different part of the city asked me to lunch. He asked how my project was going and I mentioned this pattern. I've never forgotten his advice. He asked do I want the credit or do I just want to get the idea adopted. Was it about me or was it about the team? It really was about the team because their success meant my success. Getting credit for my ideas yet having the team fail would not be good for my career. It was about the team. So, the manager's answer was simple. Tell Stan first.

That was not a performance appraisal. That was simply a friendly conversation over lunch, but it was one that dramatically improved my performance and my career. That took a measure of caring, but it also took patience. It was the patience of developing staff competencies over a long period of time. It was the opposite of management by yelling, expecting instant results.

Let's look at an example to illustrate this more thoroughly. Later when I joined the church leadership, I had a related experience. I was taking over as the chair of one of the committees and I attended my first-ever Cabinet meeting. That was the equivalent of our Board of Directors. The president at the time, Jennifer, decided it would be a good idea to spend a few minutes training our new chairs on how to conduct a committee meeting. I was surprised because by this time, I had 20 years of experience in business. I was a good manager, organizer, and public speaker. I could manage a meeting with my preferred Gantt charts, action items, budgets, agendas, and more. We'd do everything electronically. No paper. I was ready.

Then Jennifer counseled us to remember that on these committees you may be working with people who are in their twenties up through their late nineties. They come from diverse backgrounds. Some members had been stay-at-home parents. Some were school teachers. Some were engineers. Some were massage therapists. They had diverse backgrounds, educational levels, and skill sets. Jennifer said patience was needed above all. Everyone had a right to speak. Everyone was a volunteer and had to feel wanted. This was their church too after all. Yelling at volunteers or driving the meeting too fast meant you wouldn't have any volunteers left and this was all volunteer run.

So, I ran my first meeting. I had my agendas printed out. I left my computer at home. I allocated time for each agenda item and planned to get the meeting finished on time. Patience was needed. The first 20 minutes were spent discussing the weather. Would we get enough rain for the plants? Hopefully, it would be clear by Saturday. Then we checked in about each others' children. Then the conversation typically ranged to trips and peoples' health. At some point in time we managed to get to the agenda items. The meeting never finished on time but at the end of the meeting I was thanked for a great meeting.

Yes, church life is unique, but patience is a virtue of all good managers in any environment. Patience may come in different forms and be needed for different purposes. Sometimes it's simply needed to take the time to develop staff a little every day as my manager did many years ago. Sometimes, it's simply listening to let your employees feel wanted and valued.

That's not to say there's never a time for expediency. This is clearly true in professional life and it's also true in church life. But expediency and time to market cannot only coexist but it's imperative for good management, staff development, strong performing teams, and group cohesion. It's part of building a successful corporate culture.

Self-Awareness

An effective leader must first understand themselves. Church provides an interesting avenue for this. Sunday worship services provide two different but complementary avenues. Much of the service is meant to be contemplative, a time of prayer and inner peace. But then there is also a sermon which is usually aimed at helping us to become our better selves. It's a constant reminder for behavior modification. Yes, there are widely differing denominations with very different messaging, but it's still a call to modify or continue a set of behaviors. In our church, "Do Unto Others as You Would Have Them Do Unto You" is a common theme. The sermons are then followed by more prayerful contemplation in which one inevitably asks, am I following these messages and doing the right things. It's a constant call for self-awareness.

We've all met people who lack self-awareness. We've seen people chewing with their mouths open or using the speaker on their cell phone in a restroom. Those are people who are unconcerned with how their choices impact others. One can ask the question at what point is not caring about your impact on others a lack of awareness or perhaps they know precisely what they are doing but still don't care.

But self-awareness is more than avoiding rude behavior. It's also an ability to put yourself into someone else's shoes. Can you imagine what it might be like to live with a disability? Can you imagine what it would be like to be off a different race? Not everyone has this ability. This requires an ability to understand one's inner world, the assumptions that we make about ourselves. This requires a quiet confidence within ourselves such that we could imagine ourselves in different circumstances. I find the people who are unable to do this are the least confident in themselves. They are insecure.

Self-awareness also brings to light our inner biases. We are all biased in one way or another. It's simply important to recognize this. Biases are part of our genes and our experiences. Understanding these biases can help to predict how we may react in a situation and therefore to help navigate it more effectively.

One way to do this is to daydream. I recall reading some-where many years ago that executives who daydream are more effective leaders because these daydreams are mini scenarios and as they play through them, they can play act and try out different ideas without consequence. I thought this was a marvelous notion because I can't help but daydream. In fact, when I work through a complicated concept, I often hold pretend conversations in my mind where I am explaining the idea. I even ask myself questions and see if I can answer them. When I can answer them to my pretend audience's satisfaction, then I truly understand the concept. It's silly but effective. I can play through these conversations many differ-ent ways until I get it right.

Obviously, leaders who are self-aware have a better abil-ity to connect with their subordinates than those who simply bulldoze their way through relationships as though everything is a transaction. But there is also a downside to self-awareness. There was a wonderful scene on the hit TV show, Superstore, in which the character Amy is newly promoted to be store manager. She realizes there are security cameras hidden throughout the store with microphones. She takes to sitting in the security office watching and listening to her subordinates talk about her. She realizes they are making fun of the way she speaks, walks, conducts meetings, and more. She's crushed.

While this is a comedy TV show this can play out in real life as well. Three hundred sixty-degree performance assessments are very common. The idea behind these is that a person gets feedback from their manager above them, peers, and subordinates. In this way they can be more self-aware. As in our fictional example, when this feedback is unvarnished it can be devastating to one's confidence. Our inner world also needs a little protection. In my inner world I'm a little taller, a little skinnier, and have a little more hair than I know I really do. But silly things like this can provide a measure of confidence that's necessary to deal with criticism which will inevitably come.

Let's turn to another church life example. I remember one day when I was the moderator, the top lay leader elected position in our church. I was asked to meet for coffee by a member who didn't come very regularly. As I sat down with him, his first remark was, "I know the job you are doing is very hard." I knew the rest of the conversation was not going to be very complementary. Surely, he listed 12 things that I, and by extension the congregation, was doing poorly or was otherwise completely wrong. I disagreed with every point but felt no need to litigate every point but rather to simply clarify the major points. For instance, he disagreed with the sanctuary renovation under progress. That's fine but it wasn't my idea in the first place and the entire congregation voted for it unanimously. He wasn't there for that vote. So, I clarified a few points, but my inner world remained strongly intact. There are plenty of times that criticism will be given whether wanted or not. It's important to be sure the inner world remains strong.

Growth

Cultivating self-awareness is also an opportunity for overall growth. Take time to critically examine your actions and the results of them. Mistakes happen. That's fine but the key is to examine what happened and why. Then even critical examinations of painful subjects still allow the inner self to be protected. Replaying the scenarios in your mind looking for ways to make the outcomes better the next time is always helpful.

Seek out effective feedback. In the case of the gentleman who took me out for coffee in the previous example, there was simply nothing that would have pleased him. That was not effective feedback but rather venting. You will quickly find those who will give you good feedback and those who will simply complain about little things as in the case of the fictional Amy.

Sometimes taking advice can be hard. We all realize that. I've been told multiple times that I need to work harder on my small talk before diving into the meeting's business. My preference has always been to drive an agenda hard and leave small talk at home. That's also standard business but if you want to get to know your employees and develop connections, empathy, and your influence, then sometimes a little small talk is important. When conducting meetings now I try to be aware of how fast I am moving the meeting and I look for ways to spend more time up front with small talk, even though I hate it.

But there's more to leadership growth than simply increasing self-awareness. We must also recognize the changes all around us. This is especially true in professional life, but it's also true in church. The latter is not seen as the obligation it once was. The old ways of doing things can be off-putting to younger generations. Church leaders around the Western world are asking what changes are necessary to continue to bring new people in the door without alienating the older members.

In our professional lives things are changing, and change will only accelerate. What's looming ahead? Artificial intelligence, 3D printing, driverless vehicles, nanotechnology, gene editing, and climate change are just a few of such changes. How each of these will impact us is still unknown but as these changes accelerate toward us, we must find ways to grow as individuals and organizations.

Along with the concept of self-awareness we must also cultivate a sense of cognitive humility and flexibility. Cognitive humility means that we must accept that we don't have all of the answers. We don't know everything. We must listen to others and constantly absorb new information. After all, change is coming and therefore we cannot know all of the answers. We can protect our inner self when we remind ourselves of that fact. We cannot know everything because change is accelerating. A sense of cognitive humility and the ability to learn about new ideas will help us to grow as leaders.

Then we've all come across a person who says: "If it ain't broke don't fix it." We hear that a lot in church life. The old way was just fine. As I noted, though, we can't just replicate the past into the future. We must be flexible. This is where the concept of cognitive flexibility comes into play. Use those daydreams to run through different scenarios to proactively prepare for coming changes. Cultivating cognitive humility and cognitive flexibility will help to keep your mind agile and prepared. In this way you will be ready to lead others and help them adjust to the changes. "If it ain't broke don't fix it" should never be allowed to be repeated.

Leadership Styles

I would be remiss writing a book about leadership if I didn't address leadership styles. The field of leadership studies is filled with definitive lists of styles. For instance, Gary Yukl in his 2002 textbook called *Leadership in Organizations* calls out participative, charismatic, transformational, transactional, and authoritative. Others will call out coercive, authoritative, affiliative, democratic, pacesetting, and coaching as the definitive list. A quick Internet search will uncover: visionary, servant, autocratic, and even laissez-faire. Academics and consultants are famous for modifying names and lists and models and most of the time there is heavy overlap between them. Much has been written about the various styles and I won't reproduce them here. By their names they are fairly obvious.

The real key is that there are different styles and there is no one-size-fits-all style for all situations. The style used at the moment has to be an extension of the authentic self and also appropriate for the followers. One will switch back and forth between the various styles. For instance, in my work in the church my default style is participative. As we have minimal hierarchy, we have minimal authority and hence my style is one aimed at developing buy-in among the meeting partici-pants. I had very little authority or hard power and I therefore had to rely on the soft power of influence. The benefit of this style is precisely the notion that when participants feel they have been heard and have been involved in the decision, they will be committed even if they at first disagreed. The down-side to this leadership style is that it takes time and energy, strategic listening, and patience.

But even in a church there are situations that demand fast action and I then switch styles to authoritative. Should the report be formatted differently? Yes. Done. That's a silly example but it's sufficient to illustrate the point that there are different styles for different situations. When I teach, my default style is authoritative, and I never switch out of that. I simply tell the students what to do and there is absolutely no opportunity for collaboration. The assignment directions will not be changed, and grades will only be changed if I made a mistake. I will say that with a smile but there is no opportunity for participative leadership in that situation.

While I'll leave the definitions of each of the leadership styles to other authors, as so much has already been written, it is useful to call out servant leadership. The style was first coined by Robert Greenleaf in 1970. Considerable resources can be found at the Robert K. Greenleaf Center for Servant Leadership* and I'll quote from their website:

> The servant-leader is servant first ... It begins with the natural feeling that one wants to serve, to serve first. Then conscious choice brings one to aspire to lead. That person is sharply different from one who is leader first, perhaps because of the need to assuage an unusual power drive or to acquire material possessions ... The leader-first and the servant-first are two extreme types. Between them there are shadings and blends that are part of the infinite variety of human nature.
>
> The difference manifests itself in the care taken by the servant-first to make sure that other people's highest priority needs are being served. The best test, and difficult to administer, is: Do those served grow as persons? Do they, while being served, become healthier, wiser, freer, more autonomous, more likely themselves to become servants? And, what is the effect on the least privileged in society? Will they benefit or at least not be further deprived?

---

* https://www.greenleaf.org/what-is-servant-leadership/

A servant-leader focuses primarily on the growth
and well-being of people and the communities to
which they belong. While traditional leadership
generally involves the accumulation and exercise of
power by one at the "top of the pyramid," servant
leadership is different. The servant-leader shares
power, puts the needs of others first and helps
people develop and perform as highly as possible.

I remember discussing this concept with a friend of mine who
was a retired Army colonel. I described it as "the troops eat
first" style. He laughed at me and said, "when I was in charge,
I ate first." While servant leadership is a beautiful sentiment
and clearly has its place as with all styles of leadership, it has
to be exercised by the right person, at the right time, and with
the right followers.

Followership

The leadership style must be appropriate not only for the
leader, the situation, but also for the followers. Followership
is one of the most important concepts in leadership. It's also
a topic that is rarely addressed sufficiently. It's commonly
thought that when a new executive or manager joins an organization and begins to make changes that the employees will
immediately adjust and follow the new person.

For instance, perhaps a new CEO is hired and sets about
rewriting the mission and vision statements, as is so often the
case. A new vision statement is published, a five-year strategic plan is developed, and everyone knows what to do. What
if the employees are unable to adjust? Perhaps there was too
much change too fast. Perhaps they don't have the needed
skillset. Perhaps they realize that executives don't last long
in this organization and they will simply resist and wait for a

leadership change. A truly effective leader will understand that their proclamations are nothing but empty words if the followers do not follow.

In this chapter I described a model of a leader that is authentic, honest and transparent, humble, patient, and one that is deeply concerned about other people in the organization as a whole. There are many models of leadership. Clearly, there are leaders that choose to yell as in my government contractor example. There are leaders that choose to be bullies, harassing and denigrating the people around them, seeing the organization as a zero-sum game. They can only win if others lose. We can point to many examples of leaders who are bullies who have become very successful. Machiavelli might be proud, but in this book, I present a very different model. It's easy to think that a leader that is authentic and acts with integrity, humility, and patience is weaker than the bully, but the opposite is really true.

The major key to this model is to understand that we cannot examine a leader without also considering the followers. We must constantly ask the simple question: are the followers ready, willing, and able? If not, the leader must take extra time to prepare and nurture their abilities such that they are ready for the new challenges ahead. We'll explore this concept in more detail in the next chapter.

Chapter 3

Next Help Your Staff

Part of being a mentor is working with your staff to develop the type of work environment you want. Some people thrive on conflict. In a zero-sum worldview, if they didn't win, they must have lost. And it's true that organizations can be successful amidst considerable conflict. Many would point to Darwinian evolution as the model by which organizations should be run. My example of my previous boss Jerry fits this mold. For him, and the entire organization, yelling and arguing was simply par for the course. It was a nasty, cutthroat environment filled with political intrigue, ephemeral alliances, and sabotage. Many people loved that environment. But more people found it burned them out quickly. Personally, I found it simply unproductive. There was a significant turnover. That required significant training for all new hires. Then there was the avoidance. When Jerry was near the staff quickly found a way to be missing. Or they would jump on fake phone calls or rush to the bathroom.

Prior to that engagement I worked for another firm where the founder of the company, Kam, started the company to stoke his own ego as much as to make as much money as possible. My colleague Andy was desperate to get into

DOI: 10.4324/9781003323853-3

management. Every time a new management positioned opened Andy was invited to interview for it. Kam would give him a good indication that it was likely his. Then a few weeks later Kam would announce that an outsider was hired to take the management role. Kam took perverse delight in this. Andy eventually had enough of the tricks and quit.

There are countless examples like this. As I mentioned at the outset of the book if conflict motivates you, you have narcissistic tendencies, or your chief motivation is getting rich faster than your neighbor, then this is not the book for you. You probably wouldn't have read this far anyway. If, instead, your primary motivations are more intrinsic than extrinsic, and you take pride in building a well-oiled machine of an organization then the role of a mentor as a leader is more appropriate.

In this role it's important to understand the strengths and weaknesses of your staff and help them to emphasize their strengths, improve upon their weaknesses, and in general to become their best selves. When doing so it frees the leader up to focus on the higher-level tasks such as strategic planning and developing new ideas. There is also considerable research pointing to the benefits of fostering a work environment like this. In an aptly named article entitled, *Creating the Best Workplace on Earth*, authors Rob Goffee and Gareth Jones point to research from the Hay Group, noting that workplaces such as this lead to higher engagement among employees.[*] Those highly engaged employees are 50% more likely to exceed expectations. Firms with engaged employees have 54% better employee retention, 89% better customer satisfaction, and 4X better revenue growth. That's astounding. The authors say the key to this success is to help the employees be

---

[*] Rob Goffee and Gareth Jones, Creating the Best Workplaces on Earth: What Employees Really Require to Be Their Most Productive, *Harvard Business Review*, May 2013, pp. 98–106.

authentic – to be their best selves – and to work in an authentic work environment, meaning working with leaders who are authentic and lead with integrity.

These are precisely the areas where church life provides strong lessons.

Communications

One of these lessons is in the area of communications. Have you ever felt like you've been talking about a subject over and over again, yet somehow your employees still seem clueless about it? This is a common problem. Part of this stems from the fact that leaders may be acutely aware of an issue and will hold many conversations with various stakeholders over a period of time and so the issue is deeply understood by the leadership, but the employees may not have been engaged as deeply or perhaps at all. This is especially acute in church organizations. Let's use a rather long example from my time in the church leadership.

A typical congregational church, for instance, is structured with a leader, sometimes called a moderator, and officers such as the treasurer and clerk plus committee chair people structured as a board of directors. After that, there are the committee members. Then there are the other members of the church. The moderator and other officers may often spend months or even years working on a particular issue engaging various chairs of committees where needed as well as staff and the minister. The chair people of the committees may or may not discuss this issue with their committee members. Then it's usually unlikely that many of the church members have been engaged.

One can think of this in terms of degrees of separation. The committee chairs may be considered to be one degree separated from the leadership. Then, the committee members would be two degrees separated. Then the members of the church would be separated by a third degree. Sometimes this third degree can seem especially large.

For instance, ways to recruit more young families and hence children into the Sunday School and youth group programs have been a perennial issue at our church. Truly, this is a perennial issue for nearly all churches but especially those in the Northeast and Northwest and even more so in very small towns with small populations. This is a subject that I have been dealing with for years as a member of the church leadership. I have read various books, talked with the minister, talked with other churches, talked with staff, talked with committee chairs, and talked with many members of the congregation. I was deeply familiar with the topic and understood it thoroughly. For us, the decline in the number of young families and children is as much about time constraints as the other issues I just mentioned. Sports often occur on Sunday mornings. Then, families are traveling, busy, catching up on housework on the weekends, and sometimes simply tired. They are all valid excuses, and I've heard them all and lived them all as well. One day, I was in a meeting where a very passionate church member was very angry that we didn't have a stronger youth group program. He accused the leadership of not caring and of not having a plan. He was incensed that we hadn't taken a mission trip with the youth group in many years. How could this happen? Why do we spend money on other things but not our children? How can we be so uncaring and blind to this massive issue?

I had to take a moment to calm down and remember this notion of degrees of separation. I had lived with this issue for a number of years, but to this church member it was brand-new. To me, all of the reasons were well understood but that simply wasn't true for him. It's useful at a juncture like this to think back to the quiet ego as well. In a case like this it's not about the leader but rather the followers. They have to understand and be on board, or the organization won't function like the well-oiled machine we want.

So I began the process of explaining how we got to where we were. In fact, we had just taken a major mission trip to Guatemala two years prior but those kids had since graduated and we were waiting for the next group of children to mature to the point that they exited Sunday School and joined the youth group. We simply had a small population in our town, and it was unrealistic to expect that we would always have large numbers of children in the youth group. We had a thriving youth group when we had enough kids. We had a decent curriculum and activities as well as local service trips. This was a surprise to him.

Along with the quiet ego is a key tool called patience, which if you haven't noticed is also a theme of this book's leadership lessons. It's tempting to yell and berate the church member or employee, and while that's expedient it may not bring lasting change. Expediency will often add to problems later. Here a good leader can help change the tone of the conversation from angry or confused by patiently explaining and bringing the volunteer or employee along. The key is simply to remember that just because you understand a topic deeply and have been involved in the conversations over a long period of time with many stakeholders your employees may not have.

This brings up another interesting point. Just a few years prior to this discussion, we had a thriving youth group. When they returned from Guatemala, they had given a wonderful presentation to the entire congregation to a standing ovation, no less. So why didn't this church member know about this? Did he not attend the presentation? Had he not read the newsletters and emails? This is another key piece of communication. Just because the information is available doesn't mean it's either consumed or, moreover, internalized. We find that in the church we send weekly emails and monthly bulletins, post material on bulletin boards in the church, and also make frequent announcements every Sunday morning yet many people still miss the information. When asked, "Didn't you read the Thursday email?" The response is frequently no; I never read those. Well, there's a lot of good information there. It's often important to present the same information in multiple ways and multiple times. The old adage is that someone has to be given the information a minimum of five times to be sure that it really sinks in — and frankly sometimes that doesn't even work.

Every person is different and different people come to the organization with different backgrounds, skill sets, expectations, and abilities. As people work longer, the generational difference can be magnified.

Quiet Employees

But before we discuss the differences between generations, it's useful to take a short detour to further discuss how communications really happen in organizations. We typically think of the communications network within an organization as precisely following the organizational structure.

When I worked for a medium-sized corporation, I ran a team that had three levels of management above me. One would think that communications from the CEO would always be implemented; however, if there isn't trust in the system, then communications may be ignored.

In our corporation, the command structure was fairly typical. There was the CEO – Kam as I noted earlier – two vice presidents, my direct manager, and then my team. In addition, there were two senior advisors who had no other formal title. These were Bill and Bob. Both were very smart engineers with many years of experience. Both were inherently honest people who generally cared about the company and the people around them. In contrast the CEO had started the company not only to make money but also to fill his ego. It was not uncommon for him to take credit for other people's achievements. He even had his picture taken with a trophy for a 5K fun run when one of his employees ran and won the race. The CEO did not participate. There were two vice presidents. One was the CEO's friend, and while a very nice person was otherwise far out of his depth. The other vice president suffered an acute crisis of ethics. Little was beyond him as long as he and the CEO benefited.

When the CEO issued on order to one of the vice presidents to my manager to me and my team, we promptly ignored it. When the order went through the other vice president, we promptly ignored that too. When the order came via Bill or Bob, we acted upon it immediately. You might think us young and insubordinate and you may be right, but the point is, this is very common in organizational life.

Within any organization, there are informal communications networks that are far more important than the formal organizational structure. Understanding these informal networks is key to successful management. Borrowing terms from social media, the advisors in my prior example would be called influencers. They didn't have titles per se, but they had tremendous influence. A smart manager would recognize this and would tap their potential to guide the culture and performance of the organization.

But while in social media, influencers would be the ones tweeting or posting the most, influencers within organizations are often far quieter. They might not post on internal social networks or give many speeches, yet they may still carry considerable weight within the organization. They may not even send that many emails. Modern ways of tracking influencers rely on this kind of data. In the absence of this data, the old-fashioned method of simply talking to people is the key to uncover the informal communications network and the influencers. This takes time and energy and may seem like interesting work but does not directly contribute to the bottom line. But this book is also not about sales numbers, turnover, cost of goods sold, and so on. This is about developing the soft skills of leadership, which are so much harder than the hard skills of data analysis.

So how might one go about this process? One approach is to use a middle manager who has trust and access to employees at multiple levels. Another approach is to use consultants who are skilled at asking the right questions and connecting the dots. At one organization for which I was working the senior executive in charge hired a retired executive from another firm to simply walk around and talk to people when they were getting coffee, to sit in on meetings, to go to lunch with people, and to simply get to know them. It was amazingly effective. The time pressures of modern jobs make this process nearly impossible, but it is still powerful. If you cannot do it yourself, try to find someone warm and empathetic who can informally talk to people in a non-threatening way to attempt to discern how the informal communications network is structured and who those trusted influencers like Bill Bob may be.

There is no doubt this is the case in church life as well. Be aware that influencers can be positive influencers and negative influencers. Church life is a great example of the power of quiet conversations. In church we like to appear agreeable. We are all working together for a common set of goals. During my two years as moderator at our church, one individual was constantly working against me. He would smile and shake my hand. Then he would turn to the people in the pews next to him and whisper about whatever his grievance was that week. For instance, he complained that the Sunday School rooms were awful and dank because he heard that from someone else. Members would then approach me and ask why our leaders weren't doing anything about them. The truth was the rooms had been completely repainted, and murals from a famous local artist were now gracing the walls. The furniture was all new. The rooms were lovely. But it is easier to sow discord and repeat perceived grievances than it is to seek the truth. We see this on social media as well, and there are countless examples of influencers who are negative and even dangerous.

Understanding the informal networks in your organization is important, however difficult it may be. Tapping into the positive and constructive influencers can speed positive outcomes to initiatives in your organization.

Generations

Let's return to our topic of generational differences in the workplace. Bloomberg News reports that US seniors beyond the age of 70 are working at the highest rate in 55 years:

> A number of factors are keeping older Americans in the workforce. Many are healthier and living longer than previous generations. Some decide not to fully retire because they enjoy their jobs or just want to stay active and alert.
>
> Others need the money. The longer you work, the easier it is to afford a comfortable retirement. Longer lives and rising health care costs have made retirement more expensive at the same time that stagnant wages and the decline of the traditional pension have made it harder to save enough.
>
> The U.S. isn't the only place people are planning to work longer. Around the globe, workers of all ages are moving their retirement goals later and later in life.[*]

---

[*] https://www.bloomberg.com/news/articles/2017-07-10/working-past-70-americans
-can-t-seem-to-retire

Many are also semi-retired, perhaps working part time but still an active part of the labor force. Many see continued work as a key to cognitive health and even longer life. Several studies have pointed toward continued work, or volunteering, as a way to live longer.* This means that workplace teams may be made up of more generations than in the past, and this brings some unique challenges.

Much has been written on the differences between the generations, so I won't spend too much time here, but a quick review is still in order. The Greatest Generation, born between 1901 and 1924, is unlikely to be still in the workforce. Next comes the Silent Generation from 1925 to 1942, followed by the Baby Boomers born between 1943 and 1960. Generation X follows from 1961 to 1981. Then the Millennials were born roughly between 1982 and 2000. Generation Z is the most current being born after 2000. They may very well be entering the workforce and are definitely a part of church life. It's important to note that different researchers or publications will use different years to characterize the generations, but these years form a good guideline.

People born to these generations will have had different experiences that shaped their outlook, their motivations, and even their fears. Generally:

Baby Boomers

Born between 1946 and 1964, this group is also referred to as the "Me" generation. They hold positions of power and authority, such as law firm leaders and executives. Boomers are often ambitious, loyal, work centric, and cynical. They prefer monetary rewards but also enjoy nonmonetary rewards like flexible

---

* https://www.express.co.uk/life-style/health/889730/how-to-live-longer-longevity
  -working-what-is-the-retirement-age

retirement planning and peer recognition. They also don't require constant feedback and have "all is well unless you say something" mindset.

Since Boomers are so goal-oriented generation they can be motivated by promotions, professional development, and having their expertise valued and acknowledged. Prestigious job titles and recognition like office size and parking spaces are also important to Boomers.

They can also be motivated through high levels of responsibility, perks, praise, and challenge.

It's expected that around 70 million Boomers are retired or will be soon. So, they're also paying attention to 401(k) matching funds, sabbaticals, and catch-up retirement funding.

Gen X

Generation X has around 44 to 50 million Americans who were born between 1965 and 1980. They're smaller than the previous and succeeding generations, but they're often credited for bringing work-life balance. This is because they saw firsthand how their hardworking parents became so burned out.

Members of the generation are in their 30s and 40s and spend a lot of time alone as children. This created an entrepreneurial spirit with them. In fact, Gen X'ers make up the highest percentage of startup founders at 55%.

Even if they're not starting their own businesses, Gen X'ers prefer to work independently with minimal supervision. They also value opportunities to grow and make choices, as well as having relationships with mentors. They also believe that promotions should be based on competence and not by rank, age, or seniority.

Gen X'ers can be motivated by flexible schedules, benefits like telecommuting, recognition from the boss, and bonuses, stock, and gift cards as monetary rewards

Millennials (Generation Y)

Born after 1980, the tech-savvy generation is currently the largest age group in the country. They're in their 20s and are beginning to come into their own in the workforce. They're the fastest-growing segment of today's workforce.

For some Millennials, they're content with selling their skills to the highest bidder. That means, unlike Boomers, they're not as loyal. In most cases, they have no problem jumping from one organization to another.

That's not to say that you can't motivate this generation because you can by offering skills training, mentoring, and feedback. Culture is also extremely important for Millennials.

They want to work in an environment where they can collaborate with others. Flexible schedules, time off, and embracing the latest technology to communicate are also important for Gen Y.

Millennials also thrive when there's structure, stability, continued learning opportunities, and immediate feedback. If you do offer monetary rewards, they prefer stock options.

Gen Z

This generation is right on the heels of Millennials. And they're starting to enter the workplace. Even more interesting, they make up one-quarter of America's population, making this generation larger than Baby Boomers or Millennials.

This generation is motivated by social rewards, mentorship, and constant feedback. They also want to be meaningful and be given responsibility. Like their predecessors, they also demand flexible schedules.

Other ways to motivate this generation are through experiential rewards and badges such as those earned in gaming and opportunities for personal growth. They also expect structure, clear directions, and transparency.

What's most intriguing about Gen Z'ers is that 53% prefer face-to-face communication.*

Church life is a little different than business life, but it can also be a microcosm view of the challenges coming to business. It's not unusual to work in a team or committee that encompasses every one of the above generations. For instance, when working in a church education meeting shaping the Sunday School through youth group curriculum, we had teenagers, young parents in their 30s, people in various stages of middle age, and finally people in their 70s or 80s.

Indeed, in a church committee one may not only be working with different generations but also people with vastly different backgrounds. While I was leading a team, at the church, during an organizational culture change management exercise, I looked around the room, and I had school teachers, massage therapists, engineers, lawyers, and the retired CEO of the local hospital. My plan to manage the organizational change was to instantly go to one of my favorite change management methodologies, Appreciative Inquiry. Then I planned to set up a shared folder on the web where we could manage our documents, and I'd update a Gantt chart with our progress. None of my team had heard of Appreciative Inquiry or Gantt charts. Some didn't have a computer. This is a diversity that may not quite be encountered in a normal work environment, but surely there are always people with different backgrounds and skillsets. Even if the team had taken similar training, there are still differences among people and that impacts the way they work.

Similarly, those from different generations also had very different views of what the congregation should be doing. Those who were Baby Boomers gravitated to the more traditional views of the church. It was simply expected that one

---

* https://www.inc.com/john-rampton/different-motivations-for-different-generations-of-workers-boomers-gen-x-millennials-gen-z.html

would attend Sunday service and then volunteer for a committee. Millennials were more concerned with community service or what we called faith in action as opposed to the standard Sunday service. Generation X'ers, as they so often are, were ambivalent.

One of the interesting things about working in church life is learning to deal with diversity in a new way. While writing this book, I had a stark reminder of this fact. We were in a tense meeting discussing church finances. We were going over a document prepared by one of our long-serving and most trusted members, Shirley. She had presented the numbers in a neat, cogent way, but we wanted to run some what-if scenarios against them. We had a piece of paper in front of us with the numbers. The key was that some of the numbers were calculated using formulas and so it wasn't simple addition.

Everyone started talking at once, trying to help Shirley do the math. That simply made matters worse. I managed to get everyone to stop talking for a moment, which is a challenge unto itself, and then I asked Shirley to simply run multiple scenarios with her spreadsheet on her phone and get back to us. She snapped back, "I don't know how to use a spreadsheet and I don't have time to learn. I'm going to do the math my way." She proceeded with pen and paper.

Shirley is a trusted friend of mine and a very capable person. This little story is not about her shortcomings but rather the fact that in churches people come with a wide variety of backgrounds, education levels, and skill sets. The key is to understand these and seek to leverage the different backgrounds and get the most out of each person and hence the team. It's tempting to think that in business one can screen for the right types of employees with the right skill sets during the interview process, but experience shows that even then there are still differences and to help our staff become their best selves it's important to recognize that. Be prepared to help your staff magnify their strengths and either minimize their weaknesses or find ways to develop them.

Culture

It's difficult to write a book about leadership without addressing the topic of culture. Leaders must be aware of the impact cultures have on individual and group decision-making. When we think of culture, we typically think in terms of national culture but there are other modalities that need consideration as well. Rather than approach this subject comprehensively, I'll simply note that there are a wide variety of books and consultants available but let's spend a few moments considering the different modalities and why they are important.

We'll start with national culture because that's the most obvious. But there are also transnational cultures. For instance, we think of "the West" as comprising North America, UK, Europe, Australia, New Zealand, and Japan often gets lumped into this group. The reason for Japan is that it is a fast-moving, technologically sophisticated country. Those traits are shared with the US and Europe, for instance. Using this conceptual organization, we can also think in terms of fast and slow-moving cultures. For instance, the West, as we have just characterized it, is moving very quickly into the future with technological developments like commercial space flight or gene editing. Slower-moving cultures such as the Middle Eastern nations are generally thought of as moving much slower and sometimes only grudgingly into the future.

Then moving down is size, below the national level, we can look at regional variations. The culture of New England is very different than that of the Deep South. Neither is better or worse, merely different. New Englanders might be considered brash, fast speaking, and even stoic. Southerners are typically thought of as friendly and warm. We can also think of the culture of the province of Ontario as being very different than that of Quebec, which is again different than that of Alberta. Ontario is an English-speaking province and is arguably the economic engine of Eastern Canada. Ontario is, by and large, very progressive. Quebec is a French-speaking province that is fiercely independent. Alberta is a far more conservative province than either. Again, they are not better or worse, but they are quite different in nature. Then as we move smaller, we can see differences between cities and rural areas or even town vs town. Then we move downward to organizational culture and even further to intra-organizational or business unit or departmental level and finally to individual teams. Since this book is about lessons from church, we can also point to large differences from one church denomination to another.

Why is it important to understand the different cultures? At the simplest level, this will help you to improve overall awareness and aid in better decision-making. Being aware of culture may also help you to think through the consequences of actions. For instance, if executives in an organization choose to take a political position and make it public, we need to be aware of the culture of the employees, the community in which we do business, and that of the customers.

Let's just take one quick example of the pitfalls of not understanding culture. The owners of Chick-Fil-A are famously anti-LGBTQ. They chose to make a very public stance against the community. They believed it was the morally correct thing to do, and the reader is encouraged to think for themselves. When they attempted to enter the British market, the store was besieged by angry protestors. Shortly thereafter they permanently withdrew from the UK market.*

Culture issues can play out in strange and unexpected ways. For leaders it is important to be aware of the different

---

* https://www.theguardian.com/world/2019/oct/21/chick-fil-a-outlet-reading-to-close-in-lgbt-rights-row

modalities of culture and not simply think it's only national culture. For instance, a team of engineers is likely to think in radically different terms than a team of accountants. Stereotypically the latter is more conservative than the former. Engineers tend to think in terms of innovation and continuous improvement – or at last they are supposed to! – whereas the accounting world doesn't change as quickly or as often. It's important for leaders to take time to understand the various cultures with which they are dealing. In the next section we'll take a different look at the "culture" of an individual person and the implications that may have for leadership.

Worldview

This collection of backgrounds, ages, experiences, education, and even genetic makeup color what is known as one's worldview. This heavily influences nearly everything we do. It's essentially our inner identity regardless of the persona we might try to project. At our core it is our authenticity. It is easy to describe in the abstract but very difficult to label explicitly. In politics we often speak of tribalism and worldview impacts which "tribe" we may identify with, but tribalism speaks more to the fear of being left out of the group than the worldview does. Instead one's worldview is about how we view ourselves in relation to others, our past, and our future.

I can also remember an example from my days as a government contractor. Peter was a good friend of mine. He had recently been promoted to the first rung of management. His responsibilities included nothing more and nothing less than overseeing the timecards of five employees. He was not allowed to give them tasks and performance appraisals or to otherwise direct them in any meaningful way. But he was in his early 30s, and to have the title manager conferred upon him meant that he was finally becoming successful, as we are all expected to be. A very short time later, perhaps one month, the company reorganized, eliminating the bottom rung of management. Peter kept his employment but not his title. From a functional perspective, this was a meaningless change, but it rocked Peter's image of himself, impacting his worldview.

Or consider even more powerful examples. Millennials actively blame Baby Boomers and Gen X'ers for climate change. Baby Boomers were the heroes of the 20th century along with the other generations. Now, they are the villains of the 21st century? That's pretty hard to take. Or think about immigration and the fact that in 2016 minority babies became the majority for the first time.* The intention of this book is to be apolitical, so I'll leave it to your imagination how either of these examples play out.

Let's return to another church example. Interestingly we have to be careful about how we stereotype based on generation. Worldviews are much more internal and harder to judge from the outside. My friend Eric and I were talking about potentially renovating the sanctuary in the church. It was classic, simple, and formal. There was a choir loft on the chancel with crisp white walls and dark pews. The men sat on one side and the women on the other. There was a tall pulpit on one side for the minister and a lectern on the opposite for the lay leader of the service. The organ was hidden away in the back. It was very attractive, albeit stuffy, formal, and inflexible. Eric had recently been to his son's church, where the front of their sanctuary was clear and open. The minister walked around with a wireless microphone and could interact with the congregation. There were chairs for the choir instead of pews. They didn't wear robes. There were screens onto which the words of the readings or hymns were displayed. It was

---

* http://www.pewresearch.org/fact-tank/2016/06/23/its-official-minority-babies-are
-the-majority-among-the-nations-infants-but-only-just/

thoroughly modern. Why couldn't we do something like that? He was very frustrated.

Eric was in his 90s. This was not an example of the differences between generations but rather of worldview. Eric's worldview was thoroughly modern, and changing with the times was normal and appropriate. Others were upset that we would contemplate changes at all. Some – even some half Eric's age – were rooted in a vision of the past and found change discomforting. It's not to say that one was right and the other wrong but rather to point out how important these differences are.

Attempting to understand worldviews provides a wealth of information that will help to understand the reasons for resistance to change and levers to help overcome that resistance. Employing strategic listening and patience is the key to creating a window of the worldview of others. Yes, it takes more time than barking orders, but if the goal is lasting change with employee buy-in, then that time spent upfront means less wasted time later.

Change Is Hard

In many ways I'm amazed that it's necessary to point out that change is hard. In business there is an implicit assumption that a new leader can take over an organization, set a new vision, write a new strategic plan and then all of the employees line up and simply do what they are told. It always amazes me when leaders are surprised that it doesn't work out like that. When the CEO of Exxon Mobil, one of the world's largest and most complicated companies, was appointed the American Secretary of State, Rex Tillerson immediately set about building a new vision for the Department of State, and he focused on a new strategic plan and a re-organization, the favorite tool of leaders. Re-organizations are easy, and it looks like you're making an instant impact but reorgs don't change organizational culture. Culture is too deep, too ingrained to be changed by moving boxes on an organizational chart.

Tillerson complained that he was being undermined by his subordinates. He seemed generally surprised by this. I was shocked by his surprise. This happens constantly and it's not because of some deep conspiracy, not usually anyway. It's because of organizational culture as well as individual resistance to change. We'll talk about organizational culture change in a different chapter, but here we'll talk about one of its antecedents, individual resistance. The other antecedent is group dynamics, but here we'll focus on individual resistance.

Change in church life is particularly difficult. Church represents a lot of different things such as life, death, the meaning of life, social cohesion, social life, but it also represents continuity. For many people they come to church for the rituals, those little things that are done during each service, because it helps anchor them to their past. Church life helps them to withstand the swirl and chaos of life. It reminds them of their ancestors and comforts them with the knowledge that although life is transient, they are part of something bigger. Fundamentally this is about their worldview. Mess with that sense of place, self, and comfort, and you're asking for trouble.

Could a meeting about the Sunday School curriculum really devolve into a shouting match? Of course. In churches we like to think of our better selves, meaning we try hard to agree with each other and shun conflict but even then, sometimes emotions get the better of us. I recall one meeting in particular where the Sunday School director introduced the possibility of using a different curriculum the following year. Many were in favor of it, but there were some holdouts. Upon hearing the suggestion, one person who had been a long-time Sunday School teacher reacted instantly. "I will not learn a new curriculum," she said. "If the old one was good enough to be used for the last few years it's good enough to keep using."

But what happened next was even more surprising. Another teacher launched into a very calm and reasoned but long monologue. She explained what the church was like when she was a child and how she wished we could simply go back to those days. The children's choir was so lovely, and the children lit the candles while wearing special robes and had a little pattern they performed while lighting the candles. None of this had anything to do with the Sunday School curriculum, but rather it was the sense of tradition, self, and comfort that was being challenged, albeit in a very small way. The two teachers were adamant that this was not a welcome change. They would not support it.

While this may seem unique to churches it's clearly not. That sense of self, place, tradition, and comfort makes up our worldview. That's the mental model of the world as we see it. It's heavily colored by our upbringing, experiences, education, genetics, and perceived place in the world. Ask several people about their views of climate change and you will surely get a similar reaction. There are a lot of reasons for this. Group dynamics or tribalism, at least in the US is one powerful key. We know from experience that Americans are unique in their tribal views of climate change. But another reason is that climate change challenges one's worldview.

Millennials, for instance, blame Baby Boomers and Gen X'ers for climate change. It was the policies of the 20th century that led to climate change. Coal was king in the 20th century and is the villain for the 21st. Oil- and gas-guzzling cars that helped to fuel the post-World War II economic boom are now viewed as a major part of the problem. That is a very difficult message for many people to hear. Their reactions are often one of rejection of the message, the messenger, and even of the notion of climate change in general.

The reason for this is that we all react to negative messaging with a mix of emotion and intellect. Some of us are more prone to reacting with emotion more quickly than others.

For instance, several years ago, I was flying out to a business meeting. My colleagues were already there and had planned to pick me up at the airport. I had a terrible flight with bad service and many delays. I was tired and very cranky when I arrived. Marc, Brad, and Dwayne picked me up, and off we went to the meeting. Marc made the mistake of being nice and asking how my flight was. I replied angrily, "It was terrible. The service was awful. I had just read how Singapore Air was rated number 1 in the world for customer service. I wish they could fly on our domestic routes." That's of course illegal under current law ostensibly for national security reasons. That aside, Marc reacted instantly. He turned bright red and his shoulders stiffened, and he snapped, "You want foreigners flying in the US? That's a terrible idea." I've known Marc for years, and I knew this would be fun. I smiled and said, "Many years ago people were very concerned about foreign cars being imported into the US too. By the way, Marc what kind of car do you drive?" His shoulders slumped. He knew he had already lost. He drove a Toyota. Brad drove a Toyota. Dwayne drove a Mitsubishi. I drove a Land Rover. The US was still functioning just fine.

The lesson of the story isn't about foreign competition but rather our knee jerk, emotional reactions to information we don't like. Marc is not unusual. We all do this to one degree or another. Climate change, in particular, is one of those hot-button issues to which people often react emotionally first rather than with our intellect. It's actually part of our biological makeup, part of our fight or flight response. Do we run or take some time to evaluate the threat?

But then something else interesting happens. Even after the instant emotional reaction we may continue to dig in our heels, reinforcing our position, even as additional information comes in that should otherwise negate our views. In psychology this is known as affective or motivated reasoning.

The word "affect" in this case refers to an emotionally based decision-making process. When faced with disagreeable data or information, the respondent reacts emotionally to the information rather than engaging in a careful analytical review. Think in terms of the innate fight or flight response. For instance, rather than asking if the lion will attack based on its distance, its body language, the raised hair on its back, or the presence of other prey in the immediate vicinity, it is simply best to quickly move to safer ground. While this process is clearly helpful in dangerous situations, it can work against us when rational decision-making is needed. It is, however, difficult, to discern when that may be the case.

An alternative example of motivated reasoning is an accusation that a child is using drugs. When the parent is first confronted with the opinion of a friend, they may instantly dismiss it, claiming their son or daughter couldn't possibly do such a thing. Then when presented with a second instance with more details, the parent becomes agitated and insists the other person is attempting to besmirch their child's reputation. Then when presented with yet another instance with even more details, the parent becomes enraged and decides they can no longer be friends with the other.

In the previous examples, rather than an individual taking time to make a rational analytical decision about the new information presented, they instead reacted emotionally and immediately rather than taking time to rationally examine contradictory and uncomfortable information. Individuals naturally seek a comfort zone and are therefore psychologically motivated to seek confirmation. In fact, Alan Leviton from the Harvard Medical School conducted an MRI analysis in which he noted that the pleasure centers of the brain reacted when a patient was presented with confirmatory evidence.* Therefore, affective reasoning is an entirely natural reaction but one that

---

* Alan Leviton, Motivated Reasoning, *Acta Paediatrica*, Vol. 96, 2007, p. 949.

can work against us when intellectual and rational decision-making is needed.

Returning to the example of the accusation of drug use, when the accuser might tell the parent they saw the child looking dazed and acting strange, the parent might simply discount the information noting the child didn't get a lot of sleep the night before thereby confirming their bias that their child is not using drugs. When the same accuser presents a second case of the child looking dazed, the parent might then accuse the accuser of trying to intentionally discredit the reputation of the child. In this case the parent is not only confirming their bias but also reinforcing their bias. The parent might then seek additional information about the accuser seeking to further discredit them and again reinforce their own bias.

This motivated construct might continue until the parent was presented with incontrovertible evidence such as catching the child in the act or perhaps as a result of a life-changing event they themselves experienced. For instance, the parent might attend a talk about drug use in which they learn that it is very widespread at their child's school and this might be sufficient to force the parent to re-analyze their bias. Authors Redlawsk, Civettini, and Emerson call this the affective tipping point, the point at which emotionally based (affective) reasoning gives way to rational, intellectual examination.[*]

On a more complex decision, individuals may actually construct an intellectual framework that supports their biases. Ziva Kunda does an extensive review of the literature about motivated reasoning and concludes that individuals who are "motivated to arrive at a particular conclusion [due to prior biases] attempt to be rational and construct a justification of their desired conclusion that would persuade a dispassionate

---

[*] David Redlawsk, Andrew Civettini and Karen Emmerson, The Affective Tipping Point: Do Motivated Reasoners Ever "Get it"?, *Political Psychology*, Vol. 31, No. 4, 2010, pp. 563–593.

observer."* They may do this believing that they are being objective and unaware of their biases. The classic work, *The Structure of Scientific Revolutions,* by Thomas Kuhn supports this notion as the author indicates that scientists conduct their research within a dominant paradigm and worldview and hence are biased.† They even become emotionally invested in their research and their theories. Only in the face of overwhelming evidence to the contrary or a life-changing event will they reach the affective tipping point and change their position.

Not only is this true of individuals, but it is also true of groups. In the case of climate change where the vast majority of scientists agree that climate change is occurring and a major component is anthropogenic, a large and well-funded cadre of groups is working hard to not only discredit those scientists and their theory but also build an intellectual framework into which they can confirm their worldview. Individuals within the group may have slight disagreements and their own individual biases but will seek to confirm and reinforce the group's overall worldview as a power-seeking move or even simply reaffirm their in-group status.

In *The Social Conquest of the Earth,* author E.O. Wilson notes that the in-group and out-group power dynamics is particularly important in explaining individual behavior and likely harkens back to evolutionary advantage much as the fight-or-flight response.‡ For instance, one is less likely to be eaten by the lion if one is part of a larger group. Therefore, it is important to remain part of the group and hence its dominant worldview even if the individual may have some

* Ziva Kunda, The Case for Motivated Reasoning, *Psychological Bulletin*, Vol. 108, No. 3, 1990, p. 482.
† Thomas Kuhn, *The Structure of Scientific Revolutions*, The University of Chicago Press, Chicago and London, 1996.
‡ Edward Wilson, *The Social Conquest of Earth*, Liveright Publishing Corporation, New York, 2013.

disagreements. The individual will therefore act according to the dominant worldview. This is particularly evident in politics, where individuals may vote against their individual best interest, opting instead to gain favor of the party or faction to which they owe their status. In this way, they are engaging in motivated or affective reasoning to guide their decision-making process.

This emotion-based decision-making can be strongly impacted by one's worldview. This is even evident in product preferences or policy choices that might impact future product categories. For instance, some will deride the rise of hybrid cars and mourn the loss of the dominance of big V8s, a consequence of climate change and fuel mileage policies.

It's important to help employees understand this tendency about themselves and others. Once this is recognized, employees should be encouraged to explore their own worldview and discuss this with others. This act of simple transparency will help to build trust among team members. It will also help individuals, as well as the larger group, be more prepared for potential changes. It's important to note that some people have a very difficult time being introspective in anything other than a shallow manner but even recognizing this is important.

Then when the change is proposed, employees should be encouraged to take the time to remove the emotion from the decision and examine the proposal carefully, thoroughly, and honestly. Discuss their intellectual responses among the group and begin to decide how to support the proposal.

The reason I discuss this is because it may be a new concept to many people, and labeling it can help people to manage their reaction to change. Recognizing the differences in the way we react to potential change and the differences in the way people work and think can lead to the development of higher-performing teams.

High-Performance Teams

What this all leads us to is an opportunity to build high-performance teams. Teamwork is a part of life, whether it's within a church or within a business. We may refer to them as committees or task forces, but whatever the name, they are a team. While there are a lot of books written about teamwork, it's surprising how difficult it remains to get a team to work together effectively.

High-performing teams rarely occur naturally. It's possible, of course, but more often, they require nurturing. Understanding affective reasoning is one way to nurture good intra-team behaviors. How one responds to conflict within a team is critically important. It's also important that during times of conflict, you are able to step outside of the team dynamics and outside of yourself and attempt to view the team members, including yourself, dispassionately. A consulting firm, Strategic Momentum, adds:

> Consequently, the key to creating a high-performance team lies in understanding and embodying the language-action relationship. This is critically important to building relationships, trust, gaining alignment and commitment to produce breakthrough results. In fact, accelerated value creation and the associated results is exponentially proportional to the conversational dynamics an organization is capable of achieving. What we mean by conversational dynamics is the conversational mode they use when they work together.
>
> There are two types of conversations that occur in business today. There are reactive conversations and there are collaborative conversations. Reactive conversations are driven by resistance and fear and are very wasteful in that they prevent real issues from

being discussed. Collaborative conversations help build trusting relationships, and are able to effectively deal with real issues, thus accelerating results. Reactive conversations are inauthentic and closed while collaborative conversations are open and authentic. Inauthentic conversations occur when the individuals involved are unwilling to share the private and unspoken conversation hidden behind their public one.

Inauthentic conversations appear superficial and result from a fear of negative consequences. They create no value in so far as you do not know where people stand on the issue under discussion. Closed conversations appear to be confrontational. People are willing to share their viewpoints but are not willing to listen openly to others' perspectives.

Closed conversations have some value, but only if the participants persistently work through the issues. However, a high price is paid in terms of time and stress. Open conversations begin to generate much higher value. In open conversations, participants are willing to share their data and the basis for their assessments with others to produce mutual learning.

Participants work together with mutual respect to build a shared interpretation and a shared commitment to action. Authentic conversations deal with interpersonal relationship and trust issues. Authentic conversations focus on restoring relationship and trust when breakdowns occur, to insure on-going alignment and commitment.

When a team's predominant mode of conversation is inauthentic and/or closed, we find there is a high degree of resistance, waste and fear. We see these types of conversations as reactive, producing interpersonal mush and highly dysfunctional teamwork.

Business publications and studies suggest companies that stay in this mode have higher than average turnover and lower than average business results.

When a team's predominant mode of conversation is open and/or authentic, we find they create a high degree relationship and trust resulting in higher levels of innovation and creativity. We see these types of conversation as collaborative, producing interpersonal clarity and a highly functional, high-performance team. The same business publications and studies suggest companies that stay in this mode have lower than average turnover and higher than average business results.[*]

Thinking back to the previous discussion where we explored individual worldviews, group members can also begin to think about themselves and their role in the team dynamics. Some team members will be naturally creative and bring new ideas to the table. Others will be more pensive. Others will be task-masters focused on keeping the team on schedule. Others may be more facilitative.

It's also important to help team members think through the phases of team dynamics: forming, storming, norming, and performing. It's not unusual for a new team member to push the team back into the storming phase as the team now has to think about incorporating the new skillsets and worldview. If the team begins to malfunction, ask each member to take time out and examine their role in the current dynamic. What are they doing? Why are they doing it? Taking time to answer these questions honestly and transparently will re-establish that trust and help the team return to the performing phase.

It's also important to have the right degree of cognitive diversity within the team to combat the notorious

---

[*] The Critical Steps to Building a High-Performance Team by Strategic Momentum.

groupthink where everyone simply agrees. Cognitive diversity is slightly different than diversity in general. When we think about diversity, we often think about ethnic diversity. That's a good thing by itself, but it doesn't necessarily promote cognitive diversity.

The notion of cognitive diversity is that you want different perspectives and ways of thinking. For instance, I am very process oriented and I'm always thinking about the next steps. Others are very good at being creative and connecting what would appear to be unrelated concepts. Others are very good at ensuring all of the rules are followed. Then there are the natural devil's advocates. Sometimes these people are genuinely being helpful. I'm sure we've all had the experience where there are some people who need attention and find even negative attention to be satisfying.

One problem with cognitive diversity is the ability of the manager to manage the group toward a collective goal. Not surprisingly, this requires patience. Surely appropriate goal setting is needed, but the manager must be patient and guide the disparate thinkers along even though there will be discord. I've mentioned the Transition Team before, so I'll keep this example short. There we attempted to find the most appropriate cross section of the congregation so as many views were available as possible. The result was cognitive diversity. The CEO thought very differently than the lawyer who thought very differently than the massage therapist who thought very differently than the teacher. We also had four generations represented. I can tell you that each meeting was a challenge in patience. I often felt exhausted after the meetings, but the results were spectacular. By including so much diversity, the results of our discussions were robust, deep, thoughtful, and were simply not questioned by the congregation. Instead they were seen as completely representative of the collective congregation. This takes time and effort, but cognitive diversity is one key component of high-performing teams.

Courageous Followers

One key to high-performing teams is to avoid groupthink. This occurs when team members practice reward-seeking behavior or value team cohesion over vigorous debate. This can occur in all types of organizations. When I worked as a contractor to NASA, I recall being in meetings with upper management where aspiring junior managers were loath to point out holes in the executive's plans not for fear of retribution, but they wanted to be seen as agreeable, loyal, team players even when there were clearly issues with the ideas. I recall one particular instance where the top management had taken a management retreat to develop a mission statement. So much time gets wasted on mission statements, but people insist on developing them anyway. After three days they returned triumphantly. They had developed a new mission statement. Everyone was happy with it. The truth was, it was a meaningless jumble of management buzzwords that no more guided the roles or behaviors of the employees than the absence of a mission statement did. Each top manager agreed with the CEO. Not one of them had stood up and uttered that this was a waste of time and money.

There are numerous ways to prevent groupthink such as appointing a devil's advocate for all big decisions, but a far more powerful method is to cultivate courageous followers. In 1995 Ira Chaleff coined the term in his book, The Courageous Follower: Standing Up to and for Our Leaders. Being a courageous follower is more than simply not being afraid. Many of us are not afraid to speak our minds. Many of us have the internal confidence to point out errors and issues. But as Chaleff details in his book this is about creating a participatory culture where employees are valued for their input.

> Too often, a CEO spends a whole meeting presenting a "great new idea" as a fait accompli, and then asks

if there are any problems with it. The people around
the table know he's made up his mind and doesn't
really want to hear about problems, so they don't
speak up. There is no process that invites creative
dialogue.

If a leader doesn't establish a norm of creative
challenge, and courageous follower needs to ener-
getically model and advocate it. This act can be more
productive than any challenge we make to a specific
position, behavior, or policy as it is central to a group
being in healthy, creative relationship with each other
and the leader.*

This notion of the creative challenge is different than a challenge to one's authority. Instead it is a challenge to ideas with
the intent of continuous improvement, a topic we'll return to
later. As participation in idea sharing and challenging expands
a creative culture emerges. This has potentially enormous
benefits. All leaders have strengths and weaknesses, and
creating a participatory culture can help followers to enhance
their strengths and make up for their weaknesses. When seen
from this view, courageous followers are powerful team players rather than troublemakers. Rather than appointing a single
devil's advocate, everyone plays a role which is simultaneously
supportive and challenging. A leader will now view criticism
as an honest effort to facilitate shared objectives.

This can take considerable time to cultivate, but that's why
patience was a key attribute of an effective leader. When courageous followers are cultivated, they are more likely to have
a strong commitment to the organization – rather than simply
a charismatic leader. This is important because as leadership

---

* Ira Chaleff, *The Courageous Follower: Standing Up to and for Our Leaders*,
Berrett-Koehler Publishers, San Francisco, 1995, p. 88.

inevitably changes, the organization will remain strong and vital.

Ideas are also more likely to flow in such a creative culture. This has the effect of aiding the business through the identification of potential new products and services and also fixing problems proactively. When employees are engaged in mutual sharing in a culture of trust, they are far more likely to fix the problems that would have otherwise festered.

Thinking back several years ago in the church, the leader at the time, we'll call him Dave, and the Treasurer, we'll call him Ed, simply did not like each other. Dave had a style of top-down authority. He made demands on his people, and they were expected to follow. The problem is that in a volunteer-led church there is minimal actual authority. The real power is the soft power of influence. One day Dave called Ed and told him he was hiring an outside consultant to design new financial reports because he did not like either the format or the process Ed used. Ed was angry.

The consultant arrived and requested to see all of Ed's back spreadsheets and access to all of his financial data. Begrudgingly Ed complied. The consultant proceeded to inform him of the new process and new format. At the next cabinet meeting Ed loudly reported on the consultant's fees and indicated this was a misuse of funds when finances were tight. Dave disagreed and said we would use the consultant monthly. Each month Ed repeated his distaste and unsurprisingly each month he produced the reports in the same way and format as he had done. They clashed continually.

Ed was courageous in that he had no issue standing up to Dave, but the point of this story is that the creative, sharing culture was not in place. Instead Dave viewed Ed's protestations as a threat to his (albeit limited) authority. In a creative, collaborative culture of the courageous follower, this would not have been seen as a threat but rather an honest effort to facilitate shared objectives. Instead the problem continued to fester which in part leads us to our next topic: conflict resolution.

Conflict Resolution

It's difficult for me to write this section without shaking my head. Conflict in either a business or a church setting is difficult to manage. I've been on the receiving end of bad conflict management, and I've been responsible for bad conflict management.

Many years ago, as an engineer in Washington, DC, I was working on a contract with both a new project manager and a new assistant project manager. Both were inexperienced and new to management. The project manager, Tom, was away at meetings frequently and didn't spend a lot of time with the project team. Krystal was the assistant project manager, and our relationship started out very well in the beginning. We liked each other and respected each other. We could work together well.

About four months into the project we began to hit some technical roadblocks. We were discovering that we didn't have the full set of requirements, and that meant that our design wasn't going in the right direction. We knew that there was a competing company coming up with their own design, so it was critical for us to get this right. I was the lead designer, and I repeatedly asked Krystal to clarify the requirements. I think she tried but was in over her head. I'll give her the benefit of the doubt. I'll also state for the record that while I'm convinced, I'm a very nice person, very easy going, and easy to work with, even when things get tense, not everyone would agree.

It came time to present our designs to the client. They were not pleased with our design. We were not meeting the requirements, the very ones we didn't have. What began as a civil postmortem quickly turned angry. Somehow a shouting match erupted. The next day Tom called us into the conference room for conflict resolution. He didn't want to lose either of us, and he was committed to resolving this issue. He shut the door and said, you have to work together now, shake hands and deal with it. It was simple. It was elegant. It was very quick. There seemed little recourse but to shake hands and go back to work. While I shook hands, I clearly hadn't won and couldn't continue working in an environment that asked me to produce work in that way.

After shaking hands, I went back to my desk, updated my resume, and promptly spent the next few days searching for jobs. It didn't take long to find one for more pay and far more potential. I was gone within two weeks.

This was not a successful conflict resolution. Getting people to return to civility doesn't equate to resolving a conflict.

Years later when I found myself working in the leadership of the church, we had hired a new staff person to do a sensitive and fairly tricky job. This person was well educated and experienced in church life. He was perfect. We had a written job description and contract just like one might in any business. But just like in any business, Jim had strengths and weaknesses and would grow into the job. So, there were some minor details left out or that were vague in the job description allowing him room to grow.

There is a tricky relationship between staff and committee members. Staff work in a collaborative partnership with committee members. For administrative roles they report to the minister. Thus, the expectation is that if a committee member disagrees with the performance of the staff member they are requested to take up the issue with the minister. If that was not enough to resolve the issue, a meeting of the Personnel Committee, minister, and moderator was to be called.

Very shortly our new staff person encountered difficulty with several committee members. They expected him to do certain tasks that were not in his position description. While the committee members knew this, they were unconcerned. Jim worked for the church and hence worked for the committee, so they felt free to direct him. Jim politely declined and after a few instances tempers began to flare. The committee members demanded that Jim do what they say. He wasn't doing what they wanted, and they demanded to know why he was hired.

That by itself wasn't a bad thing, but they did not follow the protocol of first talking with the minister. Instead they called Jim out publicly, not once but twice. The situation became so heated neither party felt they could work together. What made matters worse was that it was summer, and the Personnel Committee and I were taking some time to be outside rather than coming to church during the week.

One day our new hire had enough and resigned. Once word got out we threw together an emergency meeting. It was too late. The time, energy, and money we had spent searching, hiring, and working with him were wasted. Worse, our new hire had a terrible church experience and never wanted to work with us or any church ever again.

When we began to do the postmortem of this situation, we realized that the conflict resolution protocol was not written down and was not necessarily well known to all committee members. Here is another example of communications and degrees of separation. We expected everyone to be thoroughly familiar with the protocol, but they weren't. So rather than berate the committee members, we recognized this flaw and instead remained calm and I called a special meeting of the cabinet which included the chair of the committee in question. My plan was to resolve this through the development of a shared and codified conflict resolution protocol. That way we could avoid pointing fingers. Remember yelling at volunteers means they won't be volunteers much longer.

The chair of the committee in question was named Olive. Immediately after I opened the meeting and introduced our topic, she interrupted me and claimed it wasn't necessary because there had been no conflict. I indicated that clearly there had been, or our new hire wouldn't have quit and been so angry and hurt. I tried to move us past finger-pointing and noted that working in a church environment is difficult, and there is always a tricky relationship between staff and committee members. It's ok that conflicts arise, but it's how we handle them that makes the difference.

Again, Olive interrupted me that this was unnecessary because no conflict had occurred, and she could handle it on her own anyway. We began discussing the organization chart and the notion of the minister as head of staff. Again, she interrupted that this was a waste of time and nothing had happened. She said she was too nice and that conflict simply couldn't occur. I reiterated that our new hire had left bitter, disappointed, and sad. Clearly something happened but I asked that we not conduct a postmortem but move constructively toward the development of a process. Again, she interrupted that we should not have this meeting.

While I am a very patient person, especially at church, I began to lose that patience. I tried hard to maintain my calm, but she interrupted yet again. I slammed my computer shut and in a very loud, but not yelling voice, said we cannot ignore the fact that there was a conflict as a member of staff felt bullied and humiliated and quit as a result. Clearly something needs to be done better. I apologized for raising my voice. I tried to move on. She interrupted again that this was unnecessary. I raised my voice again, and the meeting began to fall apart. I was never rude, nor did I actually yell, but I had raised my voice and that was enough. I closed the meeting and said we would reconvene at another time. Olive stormed out and promptly quit the church sending inflammatory emails to everyone about me.

That's why I shake my head when thinking about conflict resolution. Here I was in a meeting discussing conflict resolution when I yelled at a volunteer. Yes, she was not a volunteer much longer.

Not all conflict has to end in termination though. Successful conflict management begins with acknowledging that conflict is not avoidable. Sometimes there will be interpersonal conflict. It's not the fact that it happened that's the issue but rather how it's handled. Then it's critically important to listen, not just to hear but to listen. As Kay Lindahl, the author of *The Sacred Art of Listening*, puts it, it's critical to listen for perspective.

There needs to be a safe space for the employee to air grievances and know that they are understood. This is more than simply taking notes during a human resources intervention. This is about actively listening to try to understand their perspective. Yes, this indeed takes time. It also takes patience, a common theme of this book, but leaders who genuinely care about their employees will take the time. It's not about being soft hearted but rather taking the time to properly solve or at least ameliorate the conflict so that the employees can get back to performing.

If possible, find a place other than your office or the conference room. Take a walk. I've found that I've been able to initiate deep, genuine conversations with the simple act of taking a walk. Not only does this immediately remove the stress of the sense of place but you're taking the time to spend with the employee shows them that you care, and that simple act will often get them to open up and share in a way they may not have otherwise.

After the walk it's time for the aggrieved parties to meet. Start by acknowledging that conflict is normal. Then acknowledge that we have a common goal and that is acknowledging that each person has a legitimate perspective and that it is now time to come together to move past this conflict, understand that there may be new ways of working together that are required, and then it is time to return to performing.

Of course, this only works if there are a small number of people involved. If there is a larger group then I resort to my favorite organizational change tool, Appreciative Inquiry. While that is an organizational change management tool but what, after all, is conflict resolution but organizational change. Rather than building a new organizational structure and culture the goal is clearly more immediate. The change is simply to move from disfunction to performance.

Appreciative Inquiry is a deceptively simple method, but it is indeed powerful. Rather than walking with each party you may need to meet with small groups at a time with an eye to an all-hands meeting toward the end of the process. The ground rules are simple. Start with the reason we are here. That reason is not to resolve the conflict but rather to build a successful organization. The conflict will get resolved in time. Next ask what each person values about the organization? What are their hopes for the future? What is possible? To build that future state, what does this group need from the other group. Then when all groups are brought together, we can agree that we have common goals and likely common needs. Then it's time to cooperatively construct that future state by agreeing on new behavior patterns.

Clearly this only works when common ground can be found. There will be cases, even in churches, where authoritarian command and control will be required. Sometimes it's simply imperative to lay down the law and firings happen for legitimate reasons. While working in Washington DC a client came to me to complain about one of my subordinates. His attitude and performance were poor. Repeated attempts to get him to improve were not working. The client wanted him gone. I took this to my manager, who made a snap decision. If our client is unhappy with this person's performance, he can no longer continue on the contract. If he can no longer continue on our contract due to poor performance, we cannot, in good conscience, pass a low performer off onto another manager's contract. He was let go the next morning after a short meeting with human resources. That was an example of leading with integrity and authority.

Throughout this book I focus on leading with authenticity and integrity to form bonds with employees in the hopes of developing a cohesive, high-performing culture that can weather difficulties and changes. Don't mistake this for being soft, however. Integrity also means standing for what is right. In the case above it was not right to pass a poor performer off to another manager. In the case of egregious conflicts, having written policies and reacting immediately and appropriately are required even when it feels a bit harsh.

Chapter 4

Then Help Your Company

Let's take this deeper and shift our perspective slightly from individuals and teams to the organization as a whole. Let's begin by returning to the church leadership experience. As we terminated our transition process we wondered how we could keep this sense of excitement and flexibility going. It's too easy to become complacent and simply go back to the way things were. Many of us began reading about ongoing evaluation processes and church 2.0 and 3.0, whatever that may mean. It's not that we weren't aware of how other churches functioned. Many of us came from elsewhere with different church backgrounds. Instead it was about a collective conversation that was becoming a part of the culture of the congregation.

The more I thought about this, the more I thought there are some serious lessons for general organizations as well. But before we get into the details of organizational culture let's step back and think about why being excited and flexible is important.

It's cliché to say that the only constant is change but it's really true. The nature of work is changing. Artificial

DOI: 10.4324/9781003323853-4

intelligence (AI) has the potential to dramatically change many jobs in ways that are difficult to predict. Our supply chains will likely be far more optimized than before, even for little items. For instance, it's already possible for smart appliances or devices to reorder supplies when they are running low. Office purchasing can be streamlined, simplified, and automated. AI will impact nearly all areas of an organization with both positive and negative impacts.

There are other forms of automation too. Will we need drivers for delivery vans or trucks in 10 years? Will there be pilots in aircraft? Autonomous ships? What happens if 3D printing becomes widespread? What if a customer can simply purchase a product online and then print it immediately? How will that impact business? Global supply chains are in for massive disruption. The business of the future is going to be very different than the business of the past. Strategic planning is going to morph into change management as companies must be agile, proactive, and resilient.

Surprisingly, that's true in church life too. Churches may not be constantly looking to roll out new products and services, although in some churches that may be true, but yet there is a need to constantly be flexible and respond to the changing needs of members.

Thinking back to the discussion about the youth group many of the meeting participants yearned for an earlier time when church attendance was expected, and hence the ranks of the youth groups swelled. With economies of scale many things become possible. Large camping trips, mission trips, or service trips are easily organized. But what happens when the youth group consists of three kids, each of whom has sports and other obligations often on Sundays? How then should the church respond to provide them with the experience they want. How to balance that off with the experience their parents want for them? We recognize that younger generations may view church very differently and wish to have different experiences whether that is on Sunday morning or throughout the year.

We started this ongoing change management process formally by launching our Transition Team. Our goal was to help the congregation move emotionally from a long-time minister and to be prepared for a new minister. That sounds easy, but it isn't. Churches are inherently emotional and even political, and members develop deep relationships with their ministers and often conflate the minister with the church itself. Members are often deeply saddened and even angered when a minister moves on. It takes considerable time to allow the congregation to heal and become ready to move on.

To help the congregation to change and be prepared for ongoing change, we launched our Transition Team and began a series of small group gatherings aimed not at communicating our plans but rather the meetings were about strategic listening. This works not only one on one but also organization wide. And it's something that needs to be ongoing. Next, we employed a classic change management technique called Appreciative Inquiry. This simple but powerful technique is useful in developing a positive vision of the organization for the future. It has proven to be an excellent tool for laying the groundwork for ongoing change. As the process unfolds, we began to layer in strategic conversations as well. This is something that can be done implicitly or explicitly, meaning the lessons from this technique can be applied to any organization regardless of whether a formal change management process is needed or not.

Appreciative Inquiry

The technique is focused on the positive attributes of the organization and the position of the organization at the time rather than focusing on problem solving. The notion is that the problems will get solved if the people can work together rather than working against one another. The process of Appreciative Inquiry is divided into four stages. These are typically called: Discovery, Dream, Design, and Destiny. I prefer to call them Desire, Dream, Design, and Deliver. In the Desire phase, participants express the desire for change. Then they identify what attributes of the organization they like the most. Then in the Dream phase, participants imagine future states for the organization. Then in the Design phase, detailed plans are drawn up. The Deliver phase is self-explanatory. It's where the plans are implemented and either succeed or fail. Let's look at each phase in more detail.

Desire

This is the most important phase for building an agile culture. It is in this phase that you establish the shared desire of the staff. For instance, in a for-profit corporation you would start by asking the employees to state why they want to be there. This sounds obvious, but there are actually deeper layers beyond the employees simply wanting a paycheck. People inherently want to do a good job. They want to be productive. They want to help the organization succeed. They want to be part of something bigger than just themselves. Truthfully, there may be employees who don't want these things, and then unless your organization is a union shop those employees are easily moved on to somewhere else.

Going back to my Transition Team example we had just been through a separation with our long-time minister. As I mentioned, this can be very painful and difficult for many church members. They may have had a very special bond with the minister that goes beyond simple friendship. It takes time to move to the next stage of growth. During this phase, we employed strategic listening to hear people's stories and emotions. Next, we asked them why they had come to this particular church in the first place. Then we asked why they had continued to come. Thirdly, we asked what they wanted to see in the future.

We asked these three questions in small, intimate gatherings in people's homes with a facilitator and a note-taker. The key was the fact that we were establishing the desire of the church members to continue being members while simultaneously building a link to the Dream phase. This gave members an opportunity to think about why the church was important to them and then to give themselves permission to begin thinking about what could change. That gave them renewed ownership.

Establishing that sense of ownership in any organization helps to give people meaning. Giving them a sense that things can and will change and that they have an opportunity to impact that change helps to build energy for that change as well. Having been an employee in many organizations where it seemed nothing was going to change or instead that nothing I did would make a difference in the organization, I can attest to how powerful this feeling of ownership can be.

In this stage one can build a sense of curiosity as well. What could we change to make the working environment better? What new products or services might be possible? How can we be proactive in responding to the technological trends that could impact us? How can we use artificial intelligence to enhance rather than eliminate our own jobs? This energy, curiosity, and sense of urgency morphs Appreciative Inquiry from a change management technique to a focus on continual radical renewal. Appreciative Inquiry becomes agile inquiry.

Dream

While the Desire phase may be the most important, this phase is the most fun. This is the point at which employees can exercise their imagination. As per standard brainstorming technique, no idea is too far except for the very obvious ones. It's impossible to move one's office to Mars, for instance. The commute simply is impracticable. That type of idea should simply be ignored, but just about everything else should be fair at this point. During the Design phase, the ideas will be examined against constraints.

For the church we asked the question, what if the church burned down. What would we do then? Disband? Rebuild? Rebuild the same way or something very different? Oddly enough, I was meeting with a group of church members from around the state and they asked me to relate our Transition experience and I mentioned this question. Two people looked at me and said, "that really happened to us. Our entire church could fit into a small box since there was nothing but ashes." They rebuilt and are now stronger than ever. It was a shared sacrifice, and they moved through their Desire phase and reaffirmed their commitment. Their new church is a modest and modern building rather than a historic New England style (which isn't an actual architectural style itself but rather an evolutionary mix that generally contains at least some measure of Italianate and Gothic), but I bet their heating and maintenance costs are lower than ours.

For us, this phase was very new territory. In our business lives, brainstorming was common but that just wasn't done in church. As I mentioned one of the attractions of church for many people is the sense of tradition that anchors us to our ancestors and our world view. The idea of changing this relationship was worrisome to many and simply a foreign concept to most. In fact, I was even guilty of this myself. One day as our music committee meeting was concluding, a friend of mine mentioned that she had recently been at a different church where they had removable choir loft walls, which made their space much more flexible than ours. She wondered if it would ever be possible for us to do something similar. I audibly groaned thinking that was far too aggressive for us to even consider. Sure enough, however, as we entered the Dream phase, we began to see energy and momentum flowing around this idea. An impromptu group formed, and not long thereafter an architect was brought in to draw up the plans. A year later the money was raised, a contractor was chosen, and the work was completed to much acclaim.

Once people saw the energy and momentum flowing around the sanctuary renovation idea, new ideas started bubbling up. We had an old garden on the side of the church that had scarcely been used and was in a bit of disarray. A few people then took it upon themselves to draw up new plans for the garden, raise the money, hire a landscape architect, and complete the work. Then we also thought about how we could change over Sunday morning services just to shake things up. A few years prior that would've been a tough sell but now that we were still in the Dream phase people became excited about the possibilities. Surely enough we decided to hold the services in a different room just to see what would happen. It was exciting. Next, thoughts turned to renovating an old basement room for the children and making the conference room into a flexible space the youth group could also call their own in addition to being used for meetings. It's critically important to give people that sense of ownership and the ability to bring ideas forward.

In terms of broader organizations, employees should be encouraged to think in terms of internal core competencies as well as their customers. This allows a discussion about how to make the office a better working environment as well as what new products and services could be launched. For instance, employees always want more money but perhaps rather than straight raises, they can be encouraged to think about additional compensation schemes such as rewards for coming up with ideas that save the company money. What's important about this is that middle-management and frontline employees are closer to the core business processes and to the customers than the executives typically are. Therefore, they may actually see ideas that executives, who are otherwise charged with strategic planning, might miss.

Design

Then we enter into the design phase. Here, it's critically important that the employees understand the criteria being used to determine whether an idea is viable or not. If the criteria are not transparent, they will think that management is not open to new ideas in general, and the entire process quickly falls apart. Any energy that was built up during the previous two phases will quickly be lost. In the church, for instance, the criteria are pretty straightforward. Firstly, if someone has a great idea but can't get others to participate in the planning of that idea, meaning there simply isn't enough energy and momentum flowing around the idea, the idea quickly is abandoned. That's not really a deliberate strategy as much as it is a consequence of the way the organization functions, but nonetheless it's very transparent.

For example, in the church, I had a wonderful idea for a lobster bake fundraiser aimed at summer tourists. I called the meeting and invited participants only to find that no one was interested in helping. It was a great idea in principle but there simply wasn't energy around the idea and a large part because I had planned for August and that's vacation month. The other criteria for us, aside from money, which is always an issue for any organization, is whether the idea is so expensive or so large such as the sanctuary renovation that it needs full congregational approval. That means an all-hands meeting and a majority vote. There are a lot of good things about the congregational organizational form, but it can also be slow and cumbersome.

That doesn't have to be the case in business, of course. In fact, where possible it's useful to let the employees themselves experiment with the ideas rather than simply presenting them to management for a thumbs up or down vote. This can, however, present problems. New ideas and new ways of doing things can be disruptive. While disruptive change is sometimes good, it really depends on the nature of the organization. In information technology organizations it's common for new software to be tried out in a "sandbox" or secure network so that errant code cannot impact the regular operations. Once the code has been tested and employees have been trained, it can be safely cut into normal operations. In fact, much can be borrowed from the agile software development methodology, even in non-software firms. Extensive literature is available on agile development and project management, and I will defer to that body of knowledge rather than repeat it here.

Deliver

Finally, it's time to launch the new initiatives. Hopefully, the kinks will have been worked out in the "sandbox," but even then, that's not always the case. Amazon is one of the world's most successful companies, but even they can make mistakes. A few years ago, Amazon developed its own smartphone called the Fire Phone. The idea was brilliant. The phone came shipped with special software that allowed the owner to take an image of a product or scan a product's bar code, and the software would instantly check Amazon's databases to see if Amazon could sell it at a lower price. If so, a few clicks and the product was on its way to the phone's owner. It was brilliant. It was also a complete failure, and the company quickly stopped selling it. Some ideas are simply going to fail. The employees should feel encouraged to try new ideas out even if a failure occurs. Many employees will be scared to try lest they be punished for failure or stigmatized.

It's important at this point to return to the topic of strategic conversations. As employees are encouraged to try out new ideas, whether they fail or succeed, it's important for staff at all levels to focus on the positives rather than the negatives. After all, that is a core tenet of Appreciative Inquiry, but more than that by focusing on the positives in formal and informal communications the strategic conversations help to shape the culture of the organization. Appreciative Inquiry is a change management technique, but it doesn't have to be a one-time change. As new ideas continue to be brought forward and employees can proactively recognize the changing business climate, the organization will become an agile innovator.

In this process, the employees will play a leadership role. Remember the middle-management and line employees are closer to the business processes and customers than typical executives are. Pushing responsibility for planning and innovating further down the ladder frees up executives to look at broader trends and plan for longer-term strategies.

Shared Leadership

At this point in time there is an interesting corollary that's worth exploring. As mentioned before, congregational churches were formed as a result of crushing hierarchy. This hierarchy came in the form of a hereditary monarchy that had the power to unilaterally dictate laws and make decisions that could scarcely be challenged and certainly not at all by ordinary citizens. Those that did attempt to resist were often jailed or worse. Like-minded communities began to spring up and often found the need to flee. When they fled to the New World they were called Pilgrims.

The Pilgrim town was organized in a way that minimized hierarchy. A leader was elected from among the populace. These were the seeds of democracy. The members of the community also chose a minister rather than having one imposed on them. Decisions were made communally. The elected leadership had soft power and influence rather than hard power or authority. Their actual authority was minimal. It was critical for them to communicate ideas and proposals and seek out support from among the members of the community.

The modern congregational church functions in nearly the same way. A lay leader is elected and serves a specified term. The lay leader has nearly zero authority but has considerable soft power. Any major decision must first be vetted by the relevant committee. Then the committee chairs meet with the lay leader in what is often called a cabinet. More votes are taken. If it's a very large decision such as hiring a new minister, then the decisions must be presented to the full congregation and a vote is then taken.

One may view this as a cumbersome and slow process and indeed it is. It does have considerable upside, however. Because it requires the leader to take considerable time and not only formally present the proposal, they must also hold numerous informal conversations as this process of over communicating achieves significant buy-in. Surely there are times when the congregation-wide vote is split, but more often than not, due to the considerable communications efforts, the votes are nearly unanimous. After such a vote the organization moves forward together. The Pilgrims would feel very comfortable with this process.

Interestingly the academic literature on leadership and teams has recently seen a surge in articles about what many may consider a radical concept, *shared leadership.*

> A ... perspective that is ... gaining more adherents is to define leadership as a shared process of enhancing the individual and collective capacity of people to accomplish their work effectively. According to this perspective, leadership processes cannot be understood apart from the dynamics of the social systems in which they are embedded.

> Instead of a heroic leader who can perform all
> essential leadership functions, the functions are
> distributed among different members of the team
> or organization. Some leadership functions (e.g.,
> making important decisions) may be shared by all
> members of a group and some leadership functions
> may be allocated to individual members. Different
> people may perform a particular leadership function
> at different times. The leadership actions of any
> individual leader are much less important than the
> collective leadership provided by members of the
> organization.[*]

What this really boils down to is an organization that has little
hierarchy with shared decision-making. For instance, back to
the congregational model, the leader of the church has very
little hard authority. The decision-making rests with the moderator (lay leader) and the committee chairs. For instance, we
are thinking about repainting part of the sanctuary. I could not
unilaterally decide what the color would be. Rather, I asked
all of the chairs to begin thinking about different options and
to talk to their committee members and other members of the
congregation. Gradually a consensus bubbled up through all
of the conversations and came back as a formal recommenda-
tion. We voted on it and then acted upon. While this can be
a slow process what it ensures is the ultimate buy-in. Because
the idea was so thoroughly vetted, even though some people
might still prefer a different option, there was no pushback.
In companies, this can be compared to choosing a corporate
logo or corporate colors. The actual decision is one that is
subjective. You can research the heck out of color proposals
with marketing experts, but if you don't bring your board and

---

[*] Heifetz, 1994, as cited in Leadership in Organizations by Gary Yukl, p. 432.

employees along in the process, you could face resistance, which is detrimental to momentum.

Returning to the academic literature for a moment, this has its roots in the 1980s with discussions and experiments with self-managing teams or self-organizing teams and what Peter Senge popularized in the 1990s as the learning organization. The difference between shared leadership and self-organizing teams is the deliberate nature of this form of organizational structure. It is a deliberate choice made by the leaders to share and distribute the decision-making. It may also be considered an extreme — or even ideal – form of participative management. However, participative management generally refers to the delegation with the ability of the titular leader to override any decisions made by subordinates. Here, in the shared leadership model, the titular leader may only have the ability to override certain types of decisions or in certain circumstances. For instance, even in the case of the congregational model, the moderator has the ability to act unilaterally in the case of an emergency.

Beyond simply the ultimate form of buy-in, researchers point to several conditional benefits of shared leadership. Because shared leadership requires extensive information sharing, the team naturally develops a shared understanding of the mission, the vision, and even a shared language. One fascinating upside to this is that it obviates the tendency of some people to withhold knowledge under the old adage that knowledge is power.

How often have you seen examples of an individual or a group withholding knowledge or information, perhaps to make themselves look better in a meeting or even to sabotage someone else. For instance, several years ago, I was working as a government contractor on a very large program for one particular government agency. It was our job to rewrite all of the software to make it faster and more efficient. The client gave us all of the requirements for the software, and we began writing. Once we came to the test phase the client pointed out that the software wouldn't work because we missed key steps — that were never discussed prior to that moment. What had happened was that the client resented the fact that a contractor was given the job of writing the new software when they wanted to simply do it themselves. So, they withheld key information to make us fail. Clearly, a shared leadership model wouldn't work in this particular case, but nonetheless the point should be clear that within the shared leadership team withholding information is at least less likely to happen.

A significant amount of trust is required among the leadership team. Because of that trust, the shared understanding, and even the shared language, researchers have found that this can lead to significantly improved levels of performance in terms of productivity, agility, and the ability to change and even innovation.*

But taking this a little further, it won't be appropriate in all situations. For instance, in a telemarketing organization where there is a significant turnover of employees a shared leadership model probably doesn't make very much sense. Instead, it's more appropriate than a traditional authoritarian, hierarchical model in which the employees are told exactly what to do is more appropriate. In a slightly different example, years ago I was working with the U.S. Air Force as a government contractor to NASA on a joint mission. I was part of a team of young engineers, and we all worked extremely well together. While there was a project manager, we really functioned as a self-organizing team. We each knew what we were supposed to do, and we worked very collegially. One day we were in a meeting with some of the Air Force staff, and our team was assigned a new task. We all looked at each

---

* John Ulhoi and Sabine Muller, Mapping the Landscape of Shared Leadership: A Review and Synthesis, *International Journal of Leadership Studies*, Vol. 8, No. 2, pp. 66–87, 2014.

other and immediately began thinking about our piece of the task at how we could bring it together. One of the higher-ranking Air Force officers looked at us and said okay, who's in charge of this task. We collectively responded we are. The response was no, I need to point at "a belly button." One person has to be in charge. Clearly that was a military way of thinking but there is a valid point to be made where one person should be in charge of keeping the team on track in terms of deadlines or bringing all of the completed subtasks together to complete the job. In many ways, this is the role of the moderator in the congregational example.

How then is accountability achieved? In a typical, hierarchical authoritarian structure the leader or manager will keep track and punish or reward accordingly. In a shared leadership model, instead, it is the leadership team that will and must demand accountability from one another. Because of the shared trust in the commitment to the common mission and vision, this is generally easily achieved and will often make the participants far more accountable than would be otherwise. This is a form of an implicit reward or punishment, whereas in a traditional form of management the reward or punishment is more explicit in nature. Implicit rewards and punishments are usually far more powerful and effective.

While the shared leadership model has significant potential to enhance team performance, promote organizational agility, achieve ultimate buy-in, and even promote innovation, there can be downsides. For instance, it's critically important that all participants are ready to accept the increased responsibility that comes with sharing decisions. I recall a colleague of mine back in that previous contracting organization who came into me one day and said, "I'm really lazy. I just want to be told what to do every day and then go home at night." On the one hand, that annoyed me, but I also realized that his life was nearly stress free. That aside, however, he would not be an appropriate person to be in a shared leadership position. Thinking back to church life again, while writing this book, I was in a situation where he had a team who was tasked with coming up with ideas for the youth group. It was a small group of people, and because they were the parents of the youth group, it was imperative that they were deeply involved in the decisions that were being made on their children's behalf. That ultimate buy-in was critical to the success of the program. As we discussed the shared leadership model in this context, one person commented, "okay, I understand that is our job to come up with the ideas and then ultimately implement them, but we need someone to tell us what to do." It wasn't so much that he misunderstood the concept of shared leadership for this example, but rather he was unwilling to accept the responsibility and preferred to simply be told what to do.

In that case he did not share the commitment to the shared leadership concept. It can be difficult to shift from traditional authoritarian models to a more participative and delegative model, all the way to a fully shared leadership. Allison, Misra, and Perry noted in their 2014 article, "Doing More with More: Putting Shared Leadership into Practice," that it takes time for participants' mindsets to transform from their role as an employee or organizational leader to a culture of shared leadership.[*] Just as in Appreciative Inquiry this begins with a desire to change. It also requires an ongoing commitment to experiment and to recognize that in the beginning, decision-making may actually be less efficient until the new team norms are established prior to the next team formation stage: performing. Training, coaching, and significant self-reflection were also required to help the participants begin to see themselves in new ways. Here one may be in the Dream phase.

---

[*] Michael Allison, Susan Misra and Elissa Perry, Doing More with More: Putting Shared Leadership into Practice, April 21, 2014.

Next, organizational restructuring may be required to flatten the hierarchy. The authors above noted that organizations that undertook the move toward shared leadership often "underwent significant shifts in organizational culture and intraorganizational relationships" as authority and responsibility were distributed. This is the Design phase. Finally, the team should experiment and learn cooperatively new ways of working together in the Deliver phase.

Building a Culture of Innovation

As the team finds these new ways to work together, they establish mutual trust with themselves and with the leadership of the organization. This trust is critically important in building an agile organization that can continue to respond to the changing nature of work. It's interesting; we've talked about innovation for decades, but not only is it a topic that requires constant attention but it's also surprising how often organizations do not practice it or if they do, it's centralized as if the line employees and middle management couldn't have ideas of their own. Remember, they are closer to the business processes and customers than the executives. While the latter will have the 30,000-foot view of the organization and an understanding of the industry coupled with experience, they miss the viewpoints of the former unless they actively court it.

But there are limitations as well. I recall working for a young company as a government contractor to NASA. There was a wonderful entrepreneurial spirit in the company. Government contracting and commercial consulting are often on opposite business cycles. When the commercial sector is in a market correction or recession, the Federal Government tends to spend more. So we thought it would be great to have business in both markets. We identified potential commercial clients, met with a few, and were ready to sign the contracts.

We took the contracts to the CEO who, after much careful consideration, said no. We were still a new company, and he wanted to focus on our core client until we had enough experience and personnel to be able to expand into a different sector. He was concerned that the commercial business would be too distracting and take too much of his time away from the core client. That was a perfectly valid decision. What this points to is the need for parameters. Employees need to know what is off-limits. Innovation should not occur randomly but rather should be carefully cultivated.

There are several dimensions to creating and sustaining a culture of innovation in any organization whether for profit or even a church. Firstly, a shared understanding of innovation is needed. Innovation occurs both within the internal business processes making the organization more productive and also externally with new products and services. All too often we think of innovation as only new products, but the internal processes are also critically important. There are often ways to streamline business processes, making them more efficient, reducing waste, or reducing costs. For instance, Boeing realized they were throwing large quantities of packaging into landfills when they installed a new engine onto an airplane. They asked their engine providers to look for ways to reduce their packaging. In so doing, Boeing saved millions of dollars per year on landfill fees and eliminated tons of waste. That was a simple but important innovation. There are countless examples of these types of internal innovations. Then, of course, there are customer-facing product and service innovations. Here it is tempting to think that only breakthrough innovations are important, but even here incremental innovations, while far less exciting, can lead to increased profits.

There are many different structures organizations can use to build their innovation engines such as internal venture funds that provide funding for new ideas within the company, stage-gate product development processes which are designed to provide different levels of management support and funding at different points in the development process, focus groups, and more. There has been a lot written over the last few decades about this subject – again, it's surprising while we've been talking about the subject for so long that so few companies do this well. There are companies such as Google or 3M who are innovative at their core, but so many other companies are reactive or rely on one or two people to come up with the ideas. It's critically important that whatever internal structure is chosen that works for the particular organizational culture.

It's also critical to develop a shared understanding of the core competencies of the organization. This really starts with an understanding of the mission of the organization. That's not to say the mission statement of the organization. All too often mission statements are misleading management speak rather than a genuine attempt at characterizing what the organization really does. Next, it's important that the strategic plan is readily available and transparent as much as is practicable. Clearly there may be some sensitive areas of research and development or even parts may be withheld for security reasons, but otherwise the employees need to understand the strategy of the organization as much as possible.

Next, executive management needs to work with the employees to help them understand the core competencies of the organization. What is it that the organization does consistently well? These need to be made explicit as part of the strategic conversations. It's also important to think through what the organization does not do well. This may be an area ripe for internal innovation. Alternatively, it could be an area management wants to avoid.

Then it's critically important that innovation becomes a regular topic for meetings at all levels. This will help to regularize and institutionalize the concept. Then goals and targets need to be set, but these need to be realistic and attainable. It's easy to develop 100 ideas a month but does that really lead to meaningful innovation? It's unlikely unless a structured approach is developed whereby the employees have the help they need to take their ideas from notional to experimental to reality. This goes back to our discussion of teams. The team composition will need to demonstrate cognitive diversity. They will need a combination of pragmatists who will be quick to evaluate ideas against organization constraints such as available funding or strategic fit. These types of people are often called devil's advocates. The team should also employ angelic troublemakers who are willing to challenge the status quo and seek out new ideas. Isn't it interesting how many church-related terms apply to innovation?

Angelic troublemakers will help to challenge orthodox thinking in an organization or even an industry. They look to counter the established trends or better still exploit emerging trends before the competition. The classic example of this was the Blackberry phone vs the iPhone. Blackberries were the dominant smartphone for business because of the way they integrated with corporate information technology departments and email systems especially. They were easy to administer and use. Their keyboards were fast for emails, but their screens were small for playing games or reading the news. The maker of the Blackberry, Research in Motion, was focused like a laser on the corporate market, while Apple realized that the smartphone could be an ideal entertainment device as well as a productivity device. They spotted the trend of more and more people playing games on their phone and exploited it. The rest is history.

That's precisely the type of innovation that could occur at any level of the organization. Frontline employees were the ones principally using smartphones, and they knew precisely how they used them. Those frontline employees are also the ones closest to the customers. They have the ability to constantly look at how the customers are using the products and where things could be improved or even seek out their unarticulated needs. Steve Jobs, the late founder of Apple, was famous for saying that customer didn't know what they wanted or needed until he provided it to them. One can argue about the reality of that statement, but the notion is sound. Observing the customers from different perspectives can often lead to new insights. This is the spirit of agile inquiry.

But without metrics and accountability this could become a waste of time and resources. Metrics for innovation need to include such things as the number of dollars and employee hours spent. They should also include the number of ideas generated, the number of ideas moved to the experimental phase, and the number of ideas put into reality. Once the ideas reach the market, the classic financial metrics of cost of goods sold, profit margin, volume, and so on can be used.

It's also critically important to recognize the soft side of metrics. The idea is to build a culture of agile inquiry. How is the culture of the organization changing over time? Are employees finding the process frustrating or liberating? Are the processes clear and transparent, or do the employees feel that the criteria are arbitrary? Is the leadership acting with authenticity and integrity? Are the employees beginning to think more creatively? How has the quality of the ideas generated changed over time? When the low-hanging fruit becomes exhausted, are the employees able to move beyond into more complex ideas?

The softer side of management – dealing with people rather than simply numbers – is always the most difficult. Financial metrics are easy to review. Quality metrics such as the number of defects generated or waste produced are easy to measure. But understanding how the culture is changing requires deep strategic listening skills. This is where middle management is so important because they are closer to the frontline employees as well as the executives. Part of their job must be to listen to understand how the employees are feeling.

Back to another church example, just prior to a cabinet meeting, the minister pulled me aside and said she wanted to have a few minutes at the beginning of the meeting to ask each person how they are feeling, not about the conflict but simply about anything they wanted to share. Were they happy, frustrated, sad, mad? That is not the kind of thing normally associated with a business meeting and certainly not something I've ever experienced outside of church. No manager ever asked about my feelings before, but church is different, and as I've said at the outset of this book, there are lessons to be learned.

I have to admit I was really chafed at this idea. Church is a shared leadership structure, so I relented, and we went around the room asking about people's feelings. As we went around the room, it became clear that people were not just talking about their feelings but also reflecting on the feelings of their committee members and the other members of the church they interacted with over the last month. This became an opportunity for structured strategic listening as well as strategic conversations. As I heard the conversations, I was then able to instruct the committee chairs on how to respond and to reinforce and amplify my messages that I wrote in congregation-wide emails. It was an opportunity to reinforce the notion that we all wanted to be there, that little problems would be solved if we worked together and attempted to build the best organization we could. If we were future oriented and allowed ourselves to be flexible and experiment that the little problems would not become big problems. Our organization had had an implicit habit of pretending everything was ok because in a church there is an understanding that we should all be nice. But that meant that little problems festered and became explosions such as the one that led us to this new style of strategic listening. Had we been doing a better job of communicating before the problem, perhaps it could have been solved before it erupted. What this also required was ongoing evaluation. In a church this is more complicated than a simple performance appraisal.

Performance Appraisals

Several years ago, I was working at an Earth science satellite company. I was a contractor to them, so I had a unique view of their operations. Soon it was time for performance appraisals. One by one the employees went into their respective manager's office, and the review was conducted. It was a one-sided affair, with the manager starting off by saying nice things and then quickly delving into the employee's deficiencies. They were too frequently late to work. They were slow to learn the new processes or complained about changes too often. They didn't take the initiative. They weren't self-starters. They didn't go above and beyond whatever that meant. Most of the reviews were negative. Raises were not forthcoming.

We had a unique vantage point in this company. We were contractors flying satellites working in a computer room. We had lots of neat displays on the wall. The room was the pride of the company so it was fitted with huge windows so everyone could look in and watch us, but that meant we could also watch them. The body language said it all. No one walked away from those reviews happy. We were free to talk with them as well. They knew the performance reviews were purposely negative. It wasn't just about denying raises but moreover to justify layoffs. Shortly thereafter, security guards arrived with boxes in their hands and they went office to office removing employees and quickly escorting them out of the building so they couldn't cause any damage. It was sad and sure to be repeated at many companies.

Layoffs are an unfortunate part of business life. They are indeed sometimes necessary though. When expenses exceed revenue, the business can only function so long before something has to give. Most executives are smart enough to look for ways to both increase revenue and decrease costs without going straight for layoffs. They are a very blunt tool that can deal severe damage to morale. Morale is necessary for good performance.

The old-fashioned, lop-sided performance reviews gave way to slightly more enlightened 360-degree reviews. Here the notion was that there is a leader/follower dichotomy. It's not just about the employee's performance but also about the relationship the leader and employee have together. Is the leader providing the employee with the tools they need and the support they need to do their job effectively? So, the leader receives feedback from the employee in addition to the leader discussing the employee's performance. No leader ever wants to hear what an employee thinks of them though. Constructive criticism is rarely accepted well.

Because employees know this, they are rarely honest with their management. They will likely couch their criticism in positive terms unless the relationship is very damaged indeed. At that point the criticism will likely be biting, and a firing of the employee is likely to follow. 360-degree reviews are well intentioned but still too often used as a tool to justify withholding a raise or promotion or perhaps later for firing or layoffs. Many other performance tools have been tried, but here at the church we faced a much more complicated situation and developed a system that could be hugely valuable to business.

In a church there is a subtle, nuanced, and hugely complicated relationship between the minister, the staff, the members, and the ministries or programs of the church. This is particularly true in a congregational church where the minister serves at the pleasure of the members and therefore acts in a collaborative partnership. As I mentioned earlier in the book, the staff also have a complicated relationship with the members. The staff don't work directly for the members. They work with the members. Members cannot direct the daily work of the staff. They are, of course, free to ask questions and make suggestions, but the minister acts as head of staff and therefore the staff, administratively, report to the minister. Then, to further complicate things, the minister, staff, and members work together to maintain ministries or programs such as thrift shops or to serve the poor and homeless.

Many years ago, we struggled with this relationship. We knew something wasn't working quite right. The youth ministry was completely disconnected from the young children's Sunday School. The staff person in charge of pastoral care, coordinating visits for the ill or shut-ins, was working alone. The minister was focused on preaching and teaching evening classes. Members were frustrated. Staff were frustrated. The minister was frustrated. So, we set about evaluating the minister and the staff employing conventional performance appraisals. These were administered by a committee and largely kept confidential to save the feelings of the people involved. The committee focused principally on members' grievances and complaints and the negatives associated with the performance of the individuals and the ministries. After all, how could they improve if they didn't know what was wrong first?

The minister was so hurt by the accusations that he could barely get out of bed. He had to take a few days off to recover. When he did return, he was saddened and maddened. The chief complaint against him was that he wasn't spending enough time on his pastoral duties. He was spending too much time preaching and teaching and not enough time visiting. When he returned from his few days off, the last thing he wanted to do was to talk to people, anyone. He stayed in his office and gradually withdrew into himself, his readings, and writings. His performance got worse. Without the minister directing them, the staff were free to continue doing what they had been for better and worse. Their performance didn't change nor did the success of the ministries. Our evaluation process simply wasn't working.

A few years later and with different staff and a new minister we began to explore ways to conduct performance appraisals in a much deeper, thoughtful, careful, and thorough manner. What we developed was something we refer to as ministry review. The notion is to explore the complicated relationship between ministers, staff, members, and ministries by explicitly not focusing on individual performance but rather as a whole.

The process that we settled on was to review one-third of the church life each year and then start over. This is not a strategic planning process nor a performance appraisal but more of a deep, internal audit. Here we recognize that there is a relationship between people and processes, and it's those relationships that are the key.

If you've followed the arc of this chapter, you will have spent considerable time developing a successful culture. Hopefully, the concepts we discussed above will help to routinely refresh that culture. Next, let's talk about how to unleash this culture to make a positive difference in the world.

Chapter 5

Next Help the Earth

It has been a fun journey writing this book, and I hope you've enjoyed reading it thus far. What we are fundamentally talking about here is constantly striving to make the world a better place. That's the simple but oh-so-important message I teach children in Sunday School. It's the same message I try to impart to my graduate students. It's the same message I try to tell my children and that I try to live up to every day. But I also realize that we covered a lot of ground in a short book. So let's take a moment to review.

Concluding Remarks

Much of good leadership begins with the simple premise of authenticity and integrity. They should not be separated. Authenticity is very simply being true to yourself. It doesn't mean never changing because clearly as you grow and mature or move into new roles, you need to change. You may, for instance, be in a situation that requires you to be out of your normal character. If you're generally quiet and reserved is it ever ok to be angry? Clearly it is if you're defending a loved

DOI: 10.4324/9781003323853-5

one. This doesn't mean you're not authentic. We are all mul-
tidimensional creatures, after all. We need to adjust ourselves
as the situation demands. But we can do so without sacrificing
who we really are.

Part of the way we do this is by acting with integrity. Being
a different person in each situation would be neither authentic
nor acting with integrity. Instead, integrity means being
honest, even when no one is looking. Can one be an effective
leader while being authentic without acting with integrity? If
we're splitting hairs, yes, but that's not the type of leader I
want to be nor the type of leader I want to promote. Integrity
is a basic message of my Sunday School teachings.

People want to follow leaders who are authentic and act
with integrity. People are naturally motivated to do so. They
are also more loyal because they know the leader will back
them up. They also know that authentic leaders are also more
likely to empathize with their followers and genuinely care
about their team.

In part this is because good leaders can quiet their own
ego when necessary to listen to team members. Good leaders
surround themselves with good people and take their counsel
into consideration when making a decision.

It's not always easy to do this. It takes patience. It takes
time to get to know the team members and listen to who they
are, to their ideas, and to their needs. A good leader will not
only ask for ideas but also for constructive criticism. This is
also difficult because it can be hard to hear negative feedback.
But listening to this feedback is a way of increasing self-
awareness and a way to grow as a person and as a leader.

There are a lot of leadership assessment tools available.
These can be very interesting. Some of them are simply useful
to understand that there are differences in people. Some
people are naturally introverts which means they enjoy being
alone, and they recharge by being alone. Others are more
extroverted and prefer to be with people and find energy that

way. Most people are a mix of both and can turn them on and off. For instance, I am naturally introverted. My favorite thing to do is to read. But I can also turn on the charm and enjoy meeting new people at parties.

Other leadership assessment tools deal with different leadership styles or conflict modes. These are all useful to help you understand more about yourself and to help your team members learn about themselves as well. As a simple word of caution these tools are useful to help explain but they are not generally capable of predictive power. That means you cannot necessarily predict how someone is going to react to a given situation based on the results of an assessment tool. People are far more complicated, and a wide variety of factors may influence reactions at any one given point in time.

This brings us to a critical factor in understanding leadership. We cannot look at leadership without looking at the followers. This is what we refer to as a dyadic relationship. We cannot consider one without the others. The followers must be ready, willing, and able to follow.

New leaders entering an existing organization need to have the patience to take the time to ask questions and to engage their strategic listening skills. They must understand the followers' capabilities, needs, concerns, and desires. Only then can a healthy relationship be forged that can lead to high performance.

Along with understanding the capabilities of your followers, it's imperative to understand the limits of communication with your followers. They must be ready, willing, and able to follow you, but they must also "hear" you. It's not enough to simply state directions, but it's important to follow up to be sure they are understood and being carried out effectively. Also remember to think in terms of degrees of separation. You may give directions at the executive table, but the people separated by one degree from the executives may not get the message at all or perhaps not understand it or may willfully ignore it.

Two or more degrees of separation and the message can get watered down quickly. Think in terms of the old-fashioned telephone game. Don't make the mistake of thinking something in email will bridge the gap of the degrees of separation. We receive far too many emails, and the message may be easily muddled with all of the other information being foisted on employees.

I remember one particular employee. I would email him with three points or three questions. He would only ever respond to the first point. I didn't understand why, but for fun I started sending him three separate emails. He would respond to all three. What I came to understand later was the fact that he was dyslexic. He had trouble reading a lot of text. Short, concise messages worked for him, whereas the messages would quite literally get lost. At first, I thought he was being disrespectful. Instead, I was the problem. Remember that patience again.

Patience is especially needed when dealing with generational differences. It's exciting to think that we may have four generations in a place of work at once. Age diversity is a wonderful thing, but it does require understanding that each generation is slightly different and has slightly different attitudes. Younger people are far more likely to believe in climate change and be supportive of the LGBTQ community than Baby Boomers, for instance. Younger people also heavily value meaningful work that makes a difference in the world. It's also important to remember that generational stereotypes are simply that. Individuals will not necessarily conform to those stereotypes.

While members of the same generation may share some of the same attributes, they may differ greatly in the way they react to situations. The sum total of their genes, experiences, and education shape the way they look at the world and their place in it. Not surprisingly, this worldview is a powerful driver of behavior. It can make people react in ways that can be surprising. This is especially true when it comes to hot-button issues like climate change. Baby Boomers and Gen X'ers don't appreciate Millennials saying the former generations caused climate change, no matter how true it is. This can cause some members of the older generation to dig and resist any action on climate change or to outright deny it. They find their worldview threatened. They were the heroes of the 20th century and find themselves the villains of the 21st century. That can be very difficult to take, and so in some cases they fight back. While that's wholly counterproductive to progress, it may not matter. Remember we talked about self-awareness but not everyone practices that consciously.

Then there is the simple matter that change is difficult for some people. Some people, like me, love change. But for others change is exhausting. Not only must we avoid change for the sake of change, but we must constantly monitor the changes to see if we're being successful. As those around you see the positive effects of the changes, they will be more likely to say yes, the next time. I remember so many conversations before our Transition Team where the end result was the default answer, "that's not the way we do things here." As the Transition Team worked through the Appreciative Inquiry process, our congregation began to see the positive effects of incremental change. My friend Godfrey Comrie grew up in Jamaica. His grandfather used a phrase "every mickle makes a muckle." It's a wonderful phrase that simply means small, incremental changes can be transformational. That's certainly the case in our congregation. We were able to move from a culture of "no" to a culture of "yes," even if those changes were small and incremental. They added up.

This culture of authenticity, integrity, empathy, patience, listening, and growth – all of the topics we discussed above and in the previous chapters leads to a culture of trust. It's that culture of "yes." What's fascinating about this is that it gives teams an opportunity to experiment. If something goes wrong, we evaluate and do something else. The scientific method says observe, model, test, and try again. If you try something and it doesn't work, it's ok. Now we know that we need a different pathway. We try again. I like to tell my students that the best scientists don't know the answers. They know the questions to ask next. That's the way high-performance teams need to be. They need the trust from the leadership to know that if they fail, it's ok. Let's try something different next.

This also sets the stage for courageous followers. People need to know that they can challenge leadership without reprobation. In fact, challenge is healthy. It can lead to healthier teams that function more smoothly and as I noted with self-awareness, it can lead to leadership. Fostering a sense of trust throughout any organization leads to personal and organizational growth.

And with courageous followers challenging authority, there is bound to be conflict. That in itself is healthy. That means people are passionate enough to care. When they stop arguing we may find we have a greater problem. Acknowledge the conflict and that all parties want to be part of the solution and take time to let everyone have their voice. There are times when swift action is needed, but when promoting high-performance teams, generally patient listening is more effective.

That very step of acknowledging that all parties want to be part of the solution is the heart of a powerful change management technique called Appreciative Inquiry. The first phase, the Desire phase, starts with that very acknowledgment. It's a positivist approach meaning you don't dwell on the problems but rather, once everyone agrees to move forward, the problems will get solved along the way. The second phase is the Dream phase. It's by far the most fun. This is where you get to dream about what the organization could become if there were no constraints. It's the classic brainstorming phase. The constraints get added in the Design phase. This is where plans are drawn up, and then they are implemented in the Deliver phase.

Change management is typically thought of as a one-time event. Perhaps it is to design a new organizational structure to fit a new strategic plan or as a way of delivering new products or services. But Appreciative Inquiry can also be a principle underlying continuous change. It's a way of generating excitement about change that could otherwise be exhausting.

One way to enhance that excitement is to promote leaders within the team so that many people take responsibility for continuous change. Top-down management by diktat is needed sometimes, but for many organizations a shared leadership structure is ideal. This concept is beyond simple delegation but is about developing a sense of ownership throughout the entire organization.

For the church, that was relatively easy because it is a volunteer-led organization already. The congregation runs the church, and we work through many different committees with people rotating roles many times. This makes for a very robust structure that can and does help us deal with crises as they inevitably crop up. It can, and does, at least for the church, lead to slow action but once the action has begun, we have considerable momentum to keep it going.

The shared leadership structure also radically empowers people to come up with new ideas. At the church we say if someone has a new idea and there is excitement about it then it gets implemented. If there is little to no excitement, then it doesn't. This works well in many organizations as well, but there are often bureaucratic hurdles that tamp down that excitement too quickly. Building a culture of innovation means removing those hurdles and helping employees to develop their ideas into concrete actions. As new ideas emerge, the strategy can change accordingly. This emergent strategy can morph an organization over time into something completely new. Strategy needs to be thought of as fluid rather than strictly top-down, dictated at the annual meeting.

And finally, we must do something about the awful performance appraisals that we so often see. We need to do better. At the church we researched an overall ministerial review process where we look at the roles and actions and relationships between the volunteers and staff. What are the outcomes of the service we call a ministry? Is it working well? What needs to be done differently?

Too often in business a performance appraisal is simply a manager looking at the role of an individual in absentia of the larger organization. The manager may ask whether there is anything the company can do differently to help the individual succeed but it is not a wholistic discussion. Wouldn't it be interesting, rather than an individualized performance appraisal, to perform a team-based discussion in which the role of individuals, the team, and the company at large is initiated? It's more complicated but surely would be more meaningful.

A Message of Love and Hope

Isn't it meaning we're all seeking? On Sunday mornings, I walk into the sanctuary. I say hi to people and ask how they're doing. I check on those who have been ill. Often, I check to see if everything is working properly and help out where needed. Then I make my way to the balcony. I like to sit there, in the far back, because there is a large window in the center of the wall behind me. The sun pours through the window lighting and warming the pews.

Then the music starts and a hush comes over the congregation. This is when I begin to meditate. I forget about my To-Do list and chores around home that need to be done. I sink into the service and feel at one with the congregation.

To me, this is the special reverence that I have for church. Religion is very personal. We all approach it differently. We all have different needs at different times of our life. Sometimes we need a message of reassurance, a message that we can get through this together. Sometimes we need a simple message of love and hope. As bad as things can seem, the minister usually finds a way to weave a message of love and hope into the sermon. It may be subtle. It may be by way of a Bible story or verse. It may be a story about a child in a far-off country overcoming an obstacle. One way or another, there is usually a story of love and hope.

Then partway through the service we have a time we call Joys and Concerns. Members shout out what they are thankful for that day. Perhaps a child has come home after a tour of military duty. Perhaps so-and-so is home after a period of time in the hospital. Then there are the concerns. Someone is sick. Someone is going in for surgery.

What I find so interesting about this time of the service is the notion that we've been here before. People have gone through similar problems in the past and will again in the future. I look down and I see my friend who has multiple bouts of cancer, and despite the pain of the chemo treatments she undertook over the past week, there she is in the balcony with me. I think to myself, if she can do it, then I can also face whatever problems may get in the way of my health or happiness.

All of the people around me have gone through something similar. I'm not alone. And when I do need help these are people who will be there to help me both spiritually and physically. I take time out of my busy week to deliver meals for a sick friend. They'll do the same for me. And when we simply need to know that we're not alone there will undoubtedly be a message of love and hope ready for me.

Then there have been other times when I've entered the church when it was empty and quiet. That's not often the case as it is such a busy place. Many local groups such as two Rotary clubs rent the big room we call the Pilgrim Room.

When I do walk through the church in the quiet, it's interesting what I find. There is a brass plaque near the closet. The words have long ago rubbed off. I asked my elderly friends, and even they couldn't remember what it might have said, how old it was, or what it might have been meant to highlight. Why would someone dedicate a closet? Maybe it was meant to designate the hallway? In the distant past someone took the time to pay for it and install it. That by itself is a reminder of our ancestors. Members were here before me and will be after me.

One day I wandered into the History Room. I'm a little nosy, and I like to look around. I started digging through the pile of Annual Reports dating back decades. I read through the meeting minutes, the lists of committees, the names of the members, and the issues they were discussing. Not surprisingly, the issues were nearly identical to the issues we discuss today. They were going over the annual budget, the pledge numbers, committee rosters, and expected budget items for the upcoming year. New boilers might have been needed. The roof needed repair. The phones in the office needed updating. Annual meetings are mostly about the business of the church rather than theological discussions. They're pretty dull – then and now.

That aside, I feel connected to the previous members even though they passed away long before I was born. That brings me a sense of comfort, of continuity. I think of my parents, my grandparents, my great grandparents, and my community and its history. I feel deeply rooted and grounded. They went through many of the same things I'm going through and will face in the future.

And that makes me think of my children and potential grandchildren. How will they remember me? Will they remember me fondly? Did I make a difference in their lives and in the wider world? Yes, that message of love and hope has seeped into my being.

We are all interconnected. We are connected through our past and our future. We are connected through our community. We are connected because we are all one on this Earth under God, whatever your conception of God may be. I told you I wouldn't preach in this book.

I also remember wandering down into the original basement under the sanctuary. The building had a large addition made many years ago that house the Sunday School rooms today. The original basement is used for storage and utilities now, but the original Sunday School rooms were in this space. I wandered in ducking under the low, rough-hewn beams and into the tiny Sunday School rooms of the 19th century. It's dark and filled with spiders now. It's a little spooky, especially when the heating system turns on. It pumps hot water through the pipes to the radiators. As the pipes expand I could swear there are footsteps behind me. Then I would spin around and now I thought I hear footsteps from the other direction. I felt as though I wasn't alone even though I really was. I could almost swear to hear the voices of the children playing a hundred years ago. Back then they would have sat in their seats listening to the Bible lesson for as long as they could sit still and behave. Then no doubt someone would throw something or get up and run around. It's fun to wander around old buildings and wonder what things were like back then and think how similar things are now.

And that returns me to today and the future. I hope my descendants will think well of me. That makes me want to live well, justly, and make a positive difference in the world. Church inspires us to be our best selves. And let's be sure that message of love and hope goes beyond the sacred walls of the church. Let's take that message into the wider world.

While writing about climate change, preparing for an interfaith discussion series on the subject at the church, I came across the Seventh Generation Principle from the Iroquois Native American Nation. It says simply that every major decision must consider the impact of that decision on the next seven generations.

Imagine if corporate executives considered seven generations of people in their deliberations. Most strategic planning cycles look outward, perhaps 3–5 years. The impact on children yet to be born never enters into the discussion. How would that change the decisions?

Let's think through an example. Not long ago Australia was impacted by the worst wildfires in history. The scenes and stories were horrific. There was a tale of a family hiding indoors ready to bolt the moment the wall of fire neared the house. When they jumped into the car to flee, the tires melted. They had to jump into their other car and hope to get away. They did and lived to tell their tale. There were countless stories like this. As the fires were brought under relative control, Australians demanded the Prime Minister, Scott Morrison, enact a serious climate change mitigation strategy. Ever so reluctantly did he agree that climate change was real – he had been a devout climate change denier – and that burning coal to generate electricity was a contributor but that he would not sacrifice coal jobs. How many generations did he consider in that decision? Clearly, he was only considering the next election cycle.

A smarter decision would be to recognize that burning coal contributes to climate change and that transitioning coal miners to new jobs will take several years. Not only is training needed, but the companies with available jobs must locate in the areas where the coal miners live, or the miners need to relocate and that can lead to serious economic difficulties for local communities. A comprehensive, multiyear plan was needed. It was not forthcoming.

Perhaps their skills could have been reoriented toward working on renewable energy and hydrogen. Australia has massive renewable energy resources in wind and solar, which can mate well with hydrolyzers to split water into hydrogen and oxygen. The hydrogen can be used in fuel cell vehicles. While at this point that market is nascent, isn't that the future and isn't that the point of the Seventh Generation Principle? Let's think in terms of the impacts of our decisions on not only this generation but generations to come as well.

In the church, at the time of this writing, we're evaluating options for the repair of our steeple. The steeple is original and made from wood. Coastal Maine winters are harsh, and they take their toll on old buildings. Some of the wood is currently rotten, and the steeple needs painting as well. We're evaluating options to weatherproof the steeple by sheathing it or even completely rebuilding it out of composite materials, so our next generations of members won't have to worry about it. If we spend the extra money now, they won't have to in the future. We don't know what financial condition the congregation will be in 100 years from now. If we can afford it now, shouldn't we do so to help the congregation of the future?

Let's take this notion of reimagining a little further. In addition to worrying about the steeple our church is currently closed due to the COVID-19 pandemic. That forced us to quickly rethink our approach to Sunday service. Like many churches we used video conferencing. I quickly became the de facto producer opening the video meeting, recording, putting people on mute, and queuing up the recorded music. That allowed the minister to focus on what she does best: preaching. That helped to reduce her stress level, and she could simply concentrate on the lesson for the week.

At first, we would both go to the church and sit in the empty sanctuary, six feet apart, and run the services together. As I mentioned earlier, the building is a little creepy when it's empty and it's nice to have another person nearby. One day a bird was repeatedly banging on a nearby window. While the minister was preaching, I was able to reassure her that it wasn't a person in the hallway. It was just a bird.

In the early weeks we noticed a marked drop-off in the number of attendees. But as people figured out the technology the numbers crept up. We started connecting with people who weren't even members or were members stuck in another state because of the lockdown restrictions. Our numbers started to exceed what we would normally have if the pandemic didn't exist and we were open normally. We started to reach people who lived nearby but due to health reasons would have been unable to attend anyway. We started to see the power of video services.

One might say that was obvious since church services have been televised by other churches for decades, but we're a pretty slow-moving congregation when it comes to the sanctity of the worship service so this was a bit of a revelation for us.

We began thinking about how to keep this up even after the pandemic. The video conferencing service we were using was a bit buggy. So we contacted a local audio-visual expert. He designed a far more robust system for us. He installed a high-resolution camera in the back of the sanctuary and control equipment in a back office. We increased our internet bandwidth, and we were able to live stream services in high quality. This could also be used in video concerts, of which we have many, or weddings. Without thinking about it, we entered the 21st century.

I like to think of this as not wasting a crisis. This is such an important principle because the world faces many crises. We need messages of love, hope, and seventh-generation thinking to rise to the challenges. We cannot simply deny that challenges like climate change exist. We cannot do anything and pretend it away for the next election cycle.

What will you tell your grandchildren when they ask about what you did to address climate change? Will you look them in the eye and say, "nothing." Or worse, will you actively stand in the way of action on climate change? If you're a fervent climate change denier you probably wouldn't have read this far into the book so instead, let's address the seriousness of the situation.

Here in Maine we're already seeing impacts on our iconic lobster industry. Lobsters are staying further offshore in springtime due to increased precipitation which reduces nearshore salinity, which in turn reduces food supply. As the water warms, the cold-water-loving lobsters seek cooler waters further and further north. That's good news for Canadians but bad news for Mainers.

We're also seeing increased tick populations which are impacting deer and moose populations. This is sad in its own right, but tourists come to Maine for many reasons. One major reason is a chance to see a moose.

We also see impacts on whale populations as they shift their patterns due to warming waters. Active shipping management is required to reduce the chances of ship strikes. There are only a few hundred endangered Right Whales in the Atlantic left. Also, as the Arctic warms and it becomes a shipping route from the Atlantic to the Pacific there will be more ship strike potential there as well.

One of the other reasons tourists visit Maine is to catch sight of the colorful Puffin. These are offshore seabirds that breed on rocky islands on the coast. As the water warms the fish on which they depend are breeding earlier than the Puffins breed. As a result, the Puffin parents are catching a different species of fish that is too large for their chicks. Their population is in danger.

These are sad, but climate change is not just a local issue but also global. The church teaches us to help those in need. People around the world are and will be in need. As precipitation patterns change, agricultural patterns will change. In drought or flood-stricken areas, entire at-risk populations may be forced to move elsewhere. When they do, they will no doubt come into contact with groups that may not appreciate the influx of people. Local resources may become strained. Violence may occur.

We can expect mass migrations of people from the Middle East into Europe. We have seen this recently. We can expect this to happen again. People fleeing hurricane-stricken Puerto Rico have settled in Florida. In the islands of the South Pacific, governments are making arrangements to move their entire country to other islands – owned by other governments – or to Australia. These climate migrants are expected to increase in number. They cannot be ignored for long.

Climate change will bring many societal-level alterations. The first is simply that many people don't handle change well. As leaders, we need to be prepared to help those around us to navigate the changes and we need to do so proactively rather than reactively. We must engage our agile minds and help others to do so as well. Challenges need to be reframed as opportunities.

We must also reach out across the political aisle and across denominations. We are all in this together, and we must recognize that and act accordingly. Life is not a zero-sum game. We can succeed by helping others to succeed. Service in the name of others is true leadership. It's the spirit of the minister's message of love and hope.

Let's take time to reimagine our future. We won't go back to the way it was. There will be a constant "new normal." This can be an exciting time. Let's choose optimism over pessimism. Even if you are not the titular leader of an organization, you can lead by example.

When I teach leadership, I often use a wonderful video that reinforces this very message. The video is called "Celebrate What's Right with the World" by Dewitt Jones.* The author was a photographer for the National Geographic magazine.

---

* https://www.youtube.com/watch?v=gD_1Eh6rqf8&t=767s

He spent his career traveling around the world. National Geographic's purpose was to demonstrate beauty in everyday life around the world.

Jones tells a story of wanting to photograph a beautiful field of yellow dandelions. The lighting wasn't quite right, so he waited until the next day. When he returned to the field, the dandelions had turned to white puffballs. He missed his opportunity. Rather than despair he photographed the puffballs instead. It was a wonderful photograph he said.

He repeats a catchphrase in the video, "change your lens." It's a beautiful expression of optimism. When the photoshoot doesn't go as planned, change your lens. Choose to celebrate what's right in the world rather than what's wrong. Change your lens.

When I sit on the balcony and the sun is pouring in, I feel that message of love and hope. I feel that sense of connection to my ancestors and to my descendants, to the community around me, and to the broader world. I may be suffering but there are those around me who have experienced pain in their life, and yet there they are sitting beside me. They keep going. They may have cancer, but there they are beside me. They choose optimism. They choose to celebrate what's right with the world.

I choose optimism too. I hope you will too. Inspire those around you, and let's rise to our collective challenges together.

Appendix

About Camden, Maine

I would feel remiss if I didn't put in a plug for my adopted home, Camden, Maine. I feel privileged to be able to live in such a beautiful, vibrant community. It may be small, clinging to the sea about halfway between the Massachusetts and Canadian borders, but it's surprisingly cosmopolitan. We benefit from the retired investment bankers, spies, fund managers, and more who have settled here. We also benefit from thousands of visitors. Every summer, the size of the town triples as vacationers drive, fly, or arrive by cruise ship. If you haven't been to Maine before, you will be impressed by the entire state and especially little Camden.

All too often people think of Maine as only the home to Acadia National Park. Indeed, that is a fabulous place to visit. If you drive the coastal route north from Massachusetts, you will pass right through Camden. You may be thinking "just a couple more hours and we're there" but instead view Camden as the destination and Acadia as a day trip. Not only does the town have fabulous art galleries, music, and restaurants, but it also boasts a gorgeous harbor replete with the cutest lighthouse you will ever see, five mountains including the beautiful Camden Hills State Park with many miles of hiking trails and cliffs to climb and a ski slope all within the confines of the town.

The summer is fun as numerous schooners set sail each day with scores of tourists and kayak and paddle board rentals abound. Labor Day brings the Windjammer Festival with numerous schooners crowding the harbor, kids racing across lobster traps, lots of food, and more. Others come for stunning fall colors. The hills ringing the town come alive with oranges, yellows, and reds dotted with the green of pine trees. The chill in the air comes early, bringing thoughts of winter.

Winter is one of the best times to visit as the National Toboggan Championship is held at the ski slope known as the Snow Bowl. And if you're skiing you can see the ocean from the slopes. How often can you do that? Or join us for Christmas by the Sea when the town's tree is lit and despite the cold the streets are lined with carolers.

Or come for our famous international affairs conference, The Camden Conference. Or, how about our Camden International Film Festival. There is simply so much to do it would take a separate book to write about all of it. Fortunately, there are many guidebooks available.

Stop by. You'll enjoy it.

A Little Background on the Congregational Church

As I mentioned previously, you do not have to be religious or part of any denomination to derive value from the lessons I've identified. But I did think you might find it interesting to read a little about the congregational church in general and its roots in democratic principles. That history is alive and well. What follows is a simplified version of the official history and a little about the specifics of the church in Camden.

Many of you may never have heard of congregational churches at all. They tend to be clustered in New England, the upper Midwest, and Pennsylvania, with a smattering throughout the rest of the country. Even if you have driven by a congregational church you may know very little about them. They tend to be relatively quiet. Church members do not typically proselytize. They will not typically attempt to convert you. Instead, if you choose to join, it is of your own choosing alone. For that reason, church members are rarely outside with signs. The church also tends to be apolitical, and because the overall church has a minimal hierarchy and each individual church craves its own independence, there is some but mostly minimal coordination at the national level. This again speaks of the church being quiet on the political front. For these reasons, you may not have heard of the denomination so I thought it might be fun to explore the history a little.

The origins of the congregational church stretch back to the 1500s in England during a time of tumult and reformation. The Church of England had split with the Catholic church. The essential nature of the two churches was the same, but the former was controlled by the English king and the latter by the Pope. In each case there was an extensive hierarchy that dictated religious life not only in theological life but also in more mundane matters such as the appointment of local priests. Many people chafed at what they saw as an oppressive and unquestioning regime. In smaller churches, the quality of the appointed priests was poor and local populations wanted more control in choosing their own priests. They also wanted to exert control over the order of the service and to discipline their own church members in the way they saw fit, as opposed to having these things dictated from afar. Similar rumblings were happening throughout Europe, but congregationalism is most directly associated with the protest movement within England.

Adherents of this movement often sought to simplify the church in the areas of service as well as the church organization itself. Services of the Anglican Church of the time were elaborate affairs, and the movement sought to focus on theology rather than ceremony. They also stressed the role of the laity in the overall organization of the church. This is a central, defining feature of congregationalism today. In modern congregational churches, the laity runs the church and the minister serves at the pleasure of the congregation.

In these ways the movement sought to purify the church. They were not necessarily welcomed, however. The term "Puritan" was initially meant as a derogatory term for the movement. The movement was a challenge to the hierarchy of the Church of England, and as the king ruled the church they were viewed as a challenge to the king as well. The early movement was hence deemed illegal, and early adherents were jailed, hanged, or forced to flee. This was a time of experimentation. Early congregations, fearing persecution, would meet in people's homes. Hence an early sense of independence was developed. While they would share information, books, and a common, simplified version of Christian theology, they were far from monolithic. There were those who sought to reform the Church of England through their actions, and there were those who insisted that was impossible and a separation was needed.

Those who sought to separate completely were later called the Pilgrims. Those who sought to purify the Church of England were the Puritans. While the names are often used interchangeably today, they were originally two separate but related groups.

Because they often met in people's houses, participants would naturally choose their own leader or minister. For organizational purposes, they also chose what we would call officers today: pastor, teacher, elder, deacon, and widow. These essential functions remain today although in slightly altered form. Each church is still independent and organizes itself in the way that fits best. For instance, in my own church the organizational structure includes the moderator, the moderator-elect, the treasurer, and the clerk, all of whom are elected. The chair of the deacons, while not an officer, still exists as does the Christian education director. The widow function is instead given to the board of membership and care team. The minister, of course, serves alongside the laity. Along with the notion of choosing the leadership the participants came to the organization willingly. They were not compelled by law as they were for the Church of England. This notion of willful participation meant that everyone had an equal vote – except for women, originally.

As the groups were persecuted, one group in particular fled to Leyden, Holland. There they stayed for nearly a decade but longed for the comforts of England. They sent three petitions to the king all of which were denied. Finding life in Holland to be difficult they found an even more difficult path when they were able to convince the king they would be useful in establishing a colony in the New World. The Mayflower was being readied to establish a commercial fishery, and the Leyden Pilgrims would contribute the labor. Here they referred to themselves as Pilgrims as they were undertaking a pilgrimage of a sort to establish a free church and hopefully a free society. While underway they wrote the Mayflower Compact, which established their own method of self-government, which reflected the willful participation of the early churches.

As merchants recognized the potential of the New World, they sought additional labor hands and other disaffected groups, not all of whom would be considered a Puritan or a Pilgrim, took up the call to establish colonies.

Because the early colonists had fought the repression of a state-sponsored religion, they established a separation of church and state from the beginning. The other essential natures of modern American democracy also had seeds in the first colonies. Colonies were self-organizing, and each adult male had an equal vote. Leaders and ministers were elected rather than appointed. There was no aristocracy, and although they publicly pledged allegiance to the king, for fear of death, they sought independence at least in thought, if not fully in action, as the early years were lean times and trade with England was still needed.

Interestingly, while the early colonists were democratic in their basic nature, they were tolerant only to a point. If you agreed with the principles of the colony and the religious principles, you were welcomed. If you did not, you were banished. Women were denied a vote, and the Native Americans were persecuted as part of God's will for the chosen people. It's tempting to think of those times in idyllic terms, but clearly reality is somewhat different.

After the Mayflower, tens of thousands of colonists began to come to the New World, not all of whom were congregationalists or even those who were seeking to build a new separate or pure church and society. Later colonists often sought to continue the traditional aristocracy in the New World settling in the Mid-Atlantic and later in the South.*

The early congregational churches spread throughout Massachusetts and into all of New England and dominated religious life for a while. As the country grew the denomination grew, changed, split, and rejoined. Today congregational churches are joined by three major bodies, The United Church of Christ, The Conservative Congregational Christian Conference, and the National Association of Congregational Christian Churches. Even today the denomination continues to evolve.

---

* The different cultures that founded these regions are well described in the excellent book, *American Nations, A History of the Eleven Rival Regions of North America* by Colin Woodard. The different cultures chafed against one another then and continue to do so today.

My own church in Camden, Maine, was founded on September 11, 1805. An ecclesiastical council assembled to form a congregational church and obtain a minister. Interestingly the physical church building was built in 1799 as, by law at the time, townspeople would have to pay a fine if they didn't have a church in town. Rather than being called a church this was referred to as a meeting house. This was built in response to a fine paid in 1794. The town had to pay "two pounds, fourteen shillings, and six pence" according to the Camden town historian, Barbara Dyer, in her *History of First Congregational Church, Camden, Maine.**

The first minister was Reverend Thomas Cochran. The early years were not happy ones. After a few years people became unhappy with him and stopped coming to services. He was summarily dismissed and, as any modern American would do, promptly sued for damages. The original meeting house quickly deteriorated and was torn down in 1838. As the building was failing, church members built a new structure in 1834 for $5,000. It was dedicated in January of 1835. The original church had no organ but rather a cello to signal the note for singing. The cello is still owned by the church today, but it was replaced in 1848 when the Ladies Society purchased an organ. During this time, Rev Chapman presided. He required the utmost discipline of his members and would not tolerate dissent or criticism of his leadership. He too was dismissed. The tradition of the minister being chosen by the will of the congregation continues to this day.

Today the church continues to evolve both from the perspective of the building that is constantly being renovated and also the polity itself. Despite a general decline in religiosity nationwide and especially in New England and the Pacific Northwest, the congregation in Camden is thriving.

If you're in the area, stop by.

---

* Barbara Dyer, *History of First Congregational Church Camden, Maine*, 1991.

Index

Printed in the United States
by Baker & Taylor Publisher Services